EUROFASHION . . .

CFCC LIBRARY

EUROFASHION...
Unleashing The Designer In You

Written And Illustrated
By
Simran Preet Randhawa

Immis Publishing
Bamberg, S.C.

EUROFASHION...
Unleashing The Designer In You

By Simran Preet Randhawa

Published By:

Immis Publishing
102 Sharon St., Suite 310-A
Bamberg, S.C. 29003 U.S.A.

All rights reserved. No part of this book may be reproduced or transmitted in any form or by any means, electronic or mechanical, including photocopying, recording, or by any information storage and retrieval system without written permission from the author, except for inclusion of brief quotations in a review.

Printed and bound in the United States of America.

Copyright © 1992 by Simran Preet Randhawa.
First Printing 1992.

Publisher's Cataloging in Publication

Randhawa, Simran Preet, 1968-
  EUROFASHION...Unleashing The Designer In You/Simran Preet Randhawa.
    p. cm.
    Includes index.
    LCCN 92-70333
    ISBN 0-9631974-9-5

  1. Fashion. 2. Fashion--Popular works. 3. Consumer education.
I. Title.

TT497.R3 1992   391
                                        QB192-435

ACKNOWLEDGEMENTS

It is phenomenal to take an overview of one's life and acknowledge the multitude of people that play a role in a single life's progression. A warm feeling overcomes me when I remember the many wonderful individuals that put forth a friendly hand. Life is so short and time so quickly passing, that there is never the opportunity to reciprocate gratitude for the light each person has lit within me. For the many individuals I have come across over the years, I express my appreciation. Your thirst for information, enthusiasm, and faith are the stepping stones that kept me striving for the new and different.

Exotica International (Bamberg, S.C.) has been a primary source for these chance meetings. Thank you, Exotica, for letting me grow within your walls. I have been able to experiment, make mistakes, educate myself and others, and (hopefully) light a flame in the many lives you have allowed me to touch.

Mrs. Isabell (Boo) Sheppard, a wonderful woman that is a part of a truly beautiful family, thank you for all of the support, faith, and guidance. You have my utmost respect and love.

Extra special thanks to a few people that played a vital role in my progression: Rosilee, Gracia Dawson, Vidalia McCormick, Goodwin Brown, Ernestine Steedly, Christie Fletcher, Arthur Kohler, Joy and Larry Foster, Johnette Whetstone, Anne and Byron Tindall.

Finally and most importantly...Dear Lord, thank you for the blessings you have bestowed upon me. Thank you for the many outlets in which to express my talents. Thank you for the most fantastic parents in the world. Thank You.

Mom and Dad, Dr. and Mrs. Ajit Singh Randhawa, thank you for all of your love and support. Your belief in me is my greatest inspiration. My love for you is inexpressible.

Simran Preet Randhawa

TABLE OF CONTENTS

INTRODUCTION TO EUROFASHION

1 MENTAL BREAKDOWN: Dissecting The Designer Mind 9

2 PSYCHOLOGY OF FASHION: Realizing Your Innate Desires 23

3 COLOR-PHOBIA: Overcoming The Fear Of Color 33

4 FUTURE LIFE EXPECTANCY: Unearthing Creativity 53

5 A CLOSET CASE: Birth Of A Wardrobe 77

6 BODY SCULPTURE: Line, Illusion, And Image Formation 87

7 "FIGURE"-ATIVELY SPEAKING: Knowing Your Body 121

8 "SIZE"-MIC PROPORTIONS: Coming To Terms With Numbers .135

9 QUALITY LIVING: To Buy Or Not To Buy 139

10 HEALTHY DRESSING: A Sight For Sore Eyes 147

11 SELF-EXPRESSION: Ruling Out Myths, Legends,
And Others' Opinions...153

ILLUSTRATION INDEX 157

INDEX 161

ABOUT THE AUTHOR 171

INTRODUCTION

Hello. My name is Simran Preet Randhawa and I welcome you to my world. It is a world of fashion, color, creativity, and self-expression. It is a world where you can unlock your imagination. It is a world where you can unleash your true self and future aspirations. It is a world I want you to make your own.

I have grown up in the business of fashion and have had the chance to experience it from all angles. I am a consumer, buyer, retailer, production manager, and fashion designer. I am the average person walking down the street. I know the trials and tribulations of being thin and awkward. I understand the fears of age and feeling confined to certain styles. I am not large, but I can understand prejudice. I have been dressing size 14-24 women for ten years. I have compassion for those people that are trying so hard to please others; they do not realize they are losing themselves. I have grown up in the business. I have watched, listened, and learned; and it is my turn to give back.

Fashion is a learned process. It is an awareness issue. It is consumed through visions of what can be. This is a book bent on raising self-esteem, allowing self-expression, and opening the imagination. Some people assume these qualities as they grow older. Most people seem to lose them.

Imagination - It never ceases to amaze me...the many sources of inspiration that abound this planet. It is also interesting to see how most people miss the things that are right in front of them. By unleashing the imagination, your senses of color, clothing, styling, and decorating increase. These senses push you toward *self-expression*. Without self-expression, you are no longer individual. You are a carbon copy of those around you - a carbon copy of what society makes you. Through self-expression, you grow as a person. Through self-expression, you add to the quality of life. Through self-expression, you influence those around you. Through self-expression, you gain *self-esteem*. Every person should appreciate the individual within themselves - the individual so many of us hide from the outside world. You are a beautiful person, unconditionally. Beauty has nothing to do with race, color, size, height, or weight. Once your mind begins traveling this path of consciousness, other areas of your life are broadened.

This book, *Eurofashion...Unleashing the Designer in You*, teaches you the evolution of fashion from imagination to concept; concept to end result. You will learn new ways of mixing color, print, and fabrication. It will also make you aware of new wardrobing methods, styling methods, care and quality control and image formation.

Eurofashion is a staple of daily living. Once you understand the concepts of color, print, and fabric, you can implement these ideas into the closets of your spouse, children, parents, and/or friends. Then, home decorating can benefit from your new-found knowledge. Creativity in business will follow. The exciting elements of color, print, and texture can permeate your entire world.

SPECIAL NOTE: The information in this book is not only applicable to womenswear, but also to menswear. I urge any age to take advantage of the wonders of fashion. Feel good about yourself...You are the one that counts!

1 MENTAL BREAKDOWN:
Dissecting The Designer Mind

— What is "fashion"?

— Where does "fashion" come from?

— How do designers come up with all of those fantastic ideas?

— What will they think of next?

— What are their sources of inspiration?

Most people have a misconception about fashion: it is just clothing. THAT assumption is incorrect. Fashion is an integral part of our daily lives. Fashion is our surroundings. It affects the way we think, molds our attitudes, and expands our intelligence. Fashion is everything around us: it is clothing, cuisine, architecture; it is artistic expression; it is the way we present ourselves; it is the method by which we do things.

A breathtaking sunset can act as a catalyst for bold new colorations. A field of flowers can unearth a charismatic feeling that will inspire a new collection. World occurrences are stepping-stones into nations' cultural and ethnic background, resulting in exhibits of adoration. It is essential for every type of designer to continue churning out wonderful design. The many sources from which inspiration can be bred are inconceivable.

A designer may be influenced by buildings: the asymmetry of the Tower of Pisa, the majesty of the Taj Mahal, or the exoticism of a Russian Palace. Architectural adornments appear at random when it comes to clothing and accessory design. For example, the beautiful skyline of Manhattan has been a constant source of inspiration. (Fig. 1-1)

MENTAL BREAKDOWN: Dissecting The Designer Mind

(1-1)

The geometry of the Egyptian pyramids can be the focus of a new trend. A focus on geometry can elicit new silhouettes: trapeze, boxy, circular, tent, or flared. Then, statues and ancestral figures will be adopted for exciting new creations in accessory design. Items encompassing the realms of buttons to belts to shoes will be affected. (Fig. 1-2)

(1-2)

MENTAL BREAKDOWN: Dissecting The Designer Mind 13

(1-3)

Even the simplicity of Spanish abodes can induce an influx of ideas for fashion innovators. Clean lines, soft curves, and roof-inspired ruffles will be this designer's vocabulary. Simplicity, sophistication, and atmosphere will be the punctuation. (Fig. 1-3)

"Fashion is everything around us. It is clothing, cuisine, architecture, artistic expression, the way we present ourselves, and the method by which we do things."

The "business" of fashion is affected by all of the above. Let me take you into the mind of a designer. Let me assist you in comprehending the creative process. Marvel at the degree of focus surging through this brilliant machine.

A designer may be influenced by the way an entree is presented on a platter and the colors of the side dishes used to enhance the optics of the meal. The proportions of the servings or the way they are arranged can inspire a new design. For example, take a look at a gourmet meal and observe how it affects the mind of a designer. On this plate, there is a petite porkchop, three sprouts of broccoli protruding from the cleavage of the porkchop, pea pod halves, shrimp, carrots splayed along the plate, and a spray of bamboo shoots. Depending on the designer's specialization (sportwear, eveningwear, tailoring, men's, women's, children's), thoughts of new designs can be inspired by the optics of the arrangement. (Fig. 1-4)

(1-4)

MENTAL BREAKDOWN: Dissecting The Designer Mind 15

(1-5)

A sportswear designer may see new collar treatments, decorative detail additions, and new methods of treating fabrics. (Fig. 1-5) Model 1 is wearing a collar treatment adapted from the arrangement and shape of the pea pods. Model 2 takes on a whimsical approach, by fringing the jacket. The fringe concept came from the carrots edging the shrimp. Trapunto stitching and fabric puffing are also results of the meal. (Model 3) The trapunto stitching on the jacket is an outline of the vegetables. The fabric puffing is an adaptation of the broccoli.

A tailoring designer will use a dressier, more constructed point of view. Style line adaptation, color, and silhouette variation are just a spoonful of the ideas available. (Fig. 1-6) Notice the way the pleated skirt shoots out of the fitted covering. (Model 1) It is similar to the broccoli sprouting from the meat. Let your eyes gently caress the soft curves of Model 2. The wishbone curves are a replica of the meat's bone outline. Breathe in the aroma of color surrounding the third model. Witness the birth of an exciting new silhouette. (Model 4) Thus, many senses are aroused from just one meal.

MENTAL BREAKDOWN: Dissecting The Designer Mind

(1-6)

18   EUROFASHION: Unleashing The Designer In You

(1-7)

An eveningwear designer is allotted the satisfaction of extravagance. There are no restrictions. Bold, exciting, and extreme are the taste buds of this designer's palate. (Fig. 1-7)

MENTAL BREAKDOWN: Dissecting The Designer Mind   19

   To have the ability in deciding what inspirational choices to select from, designers must work with color analysts and print specialists. Together, they fight to keep on top of past, present, and future trends. The colors we see each season are, simply, visionary choices of our surroundings. On occasion, designers create

(1-8)

their own color cards. Our gourmet meal is a fine example. (Fig. 1-8) The colors of the entrees can influence new color combinations within an ensemble. Many designers look to nature for color inspiration. Our Lord is the most magnificent artist there ever was. Truly odd combinations can be found in His most "simple" creations: insects, flowers, vegetables, forests, the heavens.

New prints can be composed. They do not automatically appear out of thin air. In most cases, prints are derivations of textile designers. Textile designers produce the beautiful florals, paisleys, checks, plaids, and stripes that apparel designers use as technical tools. Clothing designers also design their own prints, from time to time. This practice ensures exclusivity, at least for the first season. Textile designers are also responsible for the many woven fabrications we purchase.

For a print specialist, an outside influence can result in new print design, additional color combos, or copycat prints. Print design is the use or adaptation of segments of an influence to the thoughts of the creator. (Fig. 1-9) Swatch 1 adapts shapes of the meal to carry out an existing geometric concept. Swatch 2 uses portions of the meal to establish a border for a stripe.

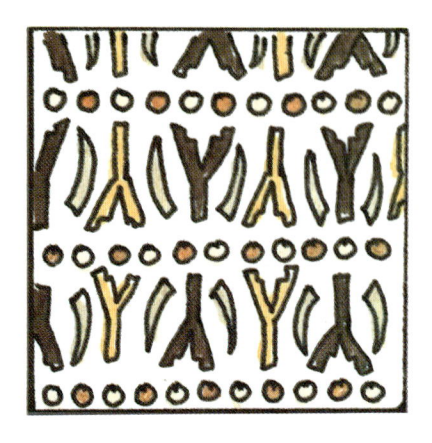

(1-9)

MENTAL BREAKDOWN: Dissecting The Designer Mind 21

An influence can introduce new combinations of color or color combos of an existing print. Swatch 1 could be re-done in shades of green with brown. It could also be made in a multi-color encompassing all colors shown on the plate. Swatch 2 could be re-introduced as just a black and white print or the entire swatch could consist of browns and oranges.

Copycat printing is the copying of the actual influence in detail. For example, swatch 3 is a print of miniature gourmet meals. Another copycat print would be of meal blowups. In this case, the plate would not be included. However, everything else would be detailed exactly. Many times, this type of printing is taken from postcards, wallpapers, and paintings.

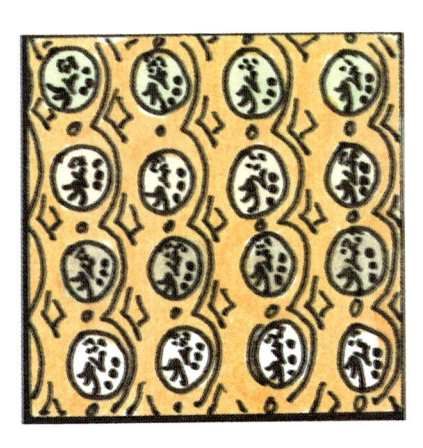

(1-9)

Our surroundings influence "the designer" to create the wonderful masterpieces in fabric. A designer's life is devotion to the exploration of new things. She/he must engage in continual education. Education leads to ideas. Ideas lead to expansion of the creative mind. Consequently, we are directly affected by the article of clothing. You may have noticed an increased awareness when around those of deeper understanding. You strive to lift your mind to theirs. The same holds true for fashion literacy. If a fashion-forward friend typically wears items of odd style and/or coloration, the practice will affect you. The more you see items of that nature, the more such variety becomes the **norm**.

You will find your purchases leaning toward a higher level of fashion consciousness. Have you every thought, "I was wearing a pant suit like that the other day. Alice is copying me. I was wearing that color combination to her party the other night. Now, she has the audacity to go out and purchase the same colors?" Perhaps an actress changes her hair color; this change will persuade some adoring fans to follow. As you can see, the latest platinum blond hair rage of the early 1990's has captured many followers - some famous and some not so famous...Madonna, Linda Evangelista, Demi Moore, the neighbor down the street. This is called the "Adoption Related Confidence" principle.

Dressing is a matter of confidence. Confidence is something that many people lack. The majority must see a style or coloration on someone else before they feel confident enough to wear it themselves. Furthermore, it is easier to adopt the fashion look if it is seen on a friend. Some people require seeing the "fashion" once before capitalizing on it. Others require many occasions to see the "fashion." You have just learned the method in which a trend catches on and fashion spreads. It is the "business" of fashion.

Fashion is a cycle of growing and changing. As time passes, the mind is fed new knowledge of what is acceptable. By broadening our minds, we can stand with confidence. By broadening our minds, we can become the designers. We have the capabilities. The tools are in our closets. The knowledge is in our hands.

2 PSYCHOLOGY OF FASHION:
Realizing Your Innate Desires

— Where does the designer start?

— Why do colors and styles change so quickly?

— Why do we accept these changes without question?

— I can't help it...when I go to the stores, I am just drawn to certain things. Why?

Through experience, I have found that people purchase "fashion" using a scale of importance: first is **coloration**; second is **print design**; and third is **silhouette**. These selections are not merely visionary choices. There is a deeper force that pushes us to select certain "fashion" items over others. The scale of importance is just an opaque covering of our subconscious and subliminally triggered mind.

Color is a most important issue. To some, it is an unbreakable barrier of daily life episodes from the physical to fashion to mental planes. To some, it is just a pretty thing to see. To others, color has meaning. Color is a channel through which we simplify life's emotions. It is a comfort zone that every person relies on, consciously or unconsciously. Color lifts us when we are down. It calms us when we are hyper. It expresses strength, sensuality, simplicity, purity, and warmth. Color can emit any feeling we wish to portray. Color is known to stimulate emotional responses: red/passion, green/love, orange/warmth, blue/calmness, white/serenity. When we see certain colors, feelings within are aroused. This response triggers a possessive need. This need in coalition with your mood of the day results in a purchase. You may recall seeing a blouse or sweater of such a beautiful color that you had to have it. This reaction is a response to which all people are sensitive. It is a response on which the fashion business thrives. This response is not accidental either. The fashion industry has conditioned us to remain eager, enthusiastic, and waiting for the next "hot" color. Fashion color experts and forecasters plan the colors designers will use each season. There are always the same colors, just variations on shade, hue, and intensity. Color, like fashion, is a cycle. Before you get too tired or attached to certain colors, new ones take their place. The new ones are colors that you, the consumer, want to see. This reality is also far from accidental. (Look at the case study below to better comprehend this cycle.)

If you think back to 1984, you will recall a surge of color in the fashion industry. Before this, browns had been dominant. The look was very nature-oriented with strength lying in leaf prints, grayed and muted florals, midwest prairie silhouettes, and natural fabrications, such as flax, cotton, and silk. The key word was COLOR. Colors were of true value. They were "crayon" colors with an almost cartoon look. In 1985, colors had a little black added to them. They were becoming deeper in intensity but still held that full blown look of color. There were no brown tinted shades anywhere, and navy was slowly fading away. Black was becoming more and more important, especially in eveningwear. In 1986, colors took on a neon glow. Seeing required sunglasses. White was more prominent than ivory. Black, black, and more black was anywhere and everywhere. 1987 brought richer, deeper colors. There was no longer the biting glow to them. Prominent colors were magenta, ruby, royal, and purple, the richer of the crayon shades. Still, there was black, black, black, and more black. In 1988, colors were intensified: magenta was fuchsia; emerald had turned into teal; and ruby became garnet. Navy had become almost nonexistent, and the future looked as if color of true value would hold strong forever. Black was King. Black was King! However, in 1989, colors had a touch of brown added to them. There was an introduction of yellows and oranges in faint hues. The colors were eggplant, burgundy, plum, and hunter green. Black continued to reign. 1990 inaugurated an influx of brown. All colors had been sauteed with brown additives. Brights were out. The colors were olive, rust, mustard, and camel. Navy was introduced as the "new" sophisticated evening color. Black was in eveningwear, however, not as strong. Color was the new "black" for evening. 1991 brought a mirage of dust colors: banana, sachet, pomander, ice blue, apricot, toast. Browns were beautiful in every shade. Most brights had an orange cast to them: lime, tangerine, mustard, aqua. Fall 1991 showed browns used every way, especially accented with shots of brights. Color had depth and magnitude. Black was a second class citizen that year. Black was the wardrobe staple and the accent piece. It was the final alternative when there was nothing else. Color was the way to go for evening: bright, rich jewels of color.

We have come full circle to the types of colors prevalent at the beginning of our case study. The colors will be close, if not identical. The story will sound familiar.

Designers use color forecasts as a guideline in coalition with their own creative forces. This is why manufacturers have such similar colors each season. Such similarity makes it easier to mix items of different brands and establish an individual image. Finding the same colors in varying fabrications is also a plus when it comes to wardrobing. Prints contain similar colors to allow for easy mixing, resulting in increased European looks.

Print design is another area that is so camouflaged by an idea that it just happens. Prints are also directed by forecasters. However, forecasters are directed by current cultural, ethical, environmental, and aesthetic world events.

(2-1)

Ethnic influences such as Indian, Oriental, and Egyptian may emerge. (Fig. 2-1) The movie *A Passage to India* inspired paisley prints and madras plaids. **The Last Emperor** reintroduced kimono-inspired embroideries.

PSYCHOLOGY OF FASHION: Realizing Your Innate Desires 27

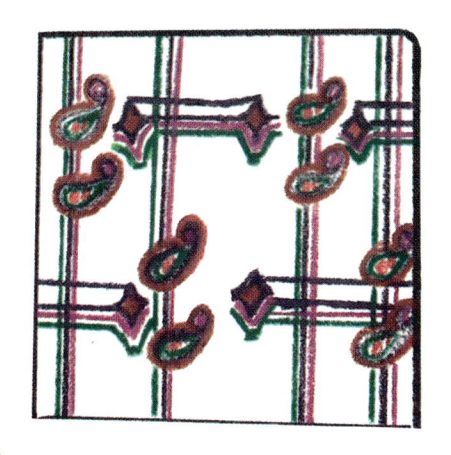

(2-1)

There can be environmental influences reflected through the use of flowers, oceans, and jungles. Contemplation of these areas of the environment will evoke thoughts of exotic new hybrids, cleaning the world's oceans, and saving the rain forests. These thoughts act as a catalyst producing exclamatory salutes to nature. This homage is the reason for the lush color and richness presented in prints of the abstract or those in detail. (Fig. 2-2 and 2-3)

(2-2)

(2-3)

There can be social conscious awareness issues that inspire. These might include protection against nuclear war, homeless causes, AIDS and education about other illnesses. (Fig. 2-4) The psychedelic sixties are remembered for their fervor and strength of life. There was a great resentment of war and a passion for the love of people and the "want" to survive. Such interests were expressed beautifully by vivid color, the freeness of styles of dress, and the homage paid to the environment by bold daisies. The daisy was an expression of clean, simple, innocent love. It represented the antithesis of every problem existing in the 1960's. Today, there are symbols to represent the same ideas but in a more controlled manner. Expressions through accessory and garment design are illustrated on the next page. Seeing examples, such as these, raises our social consciousness.

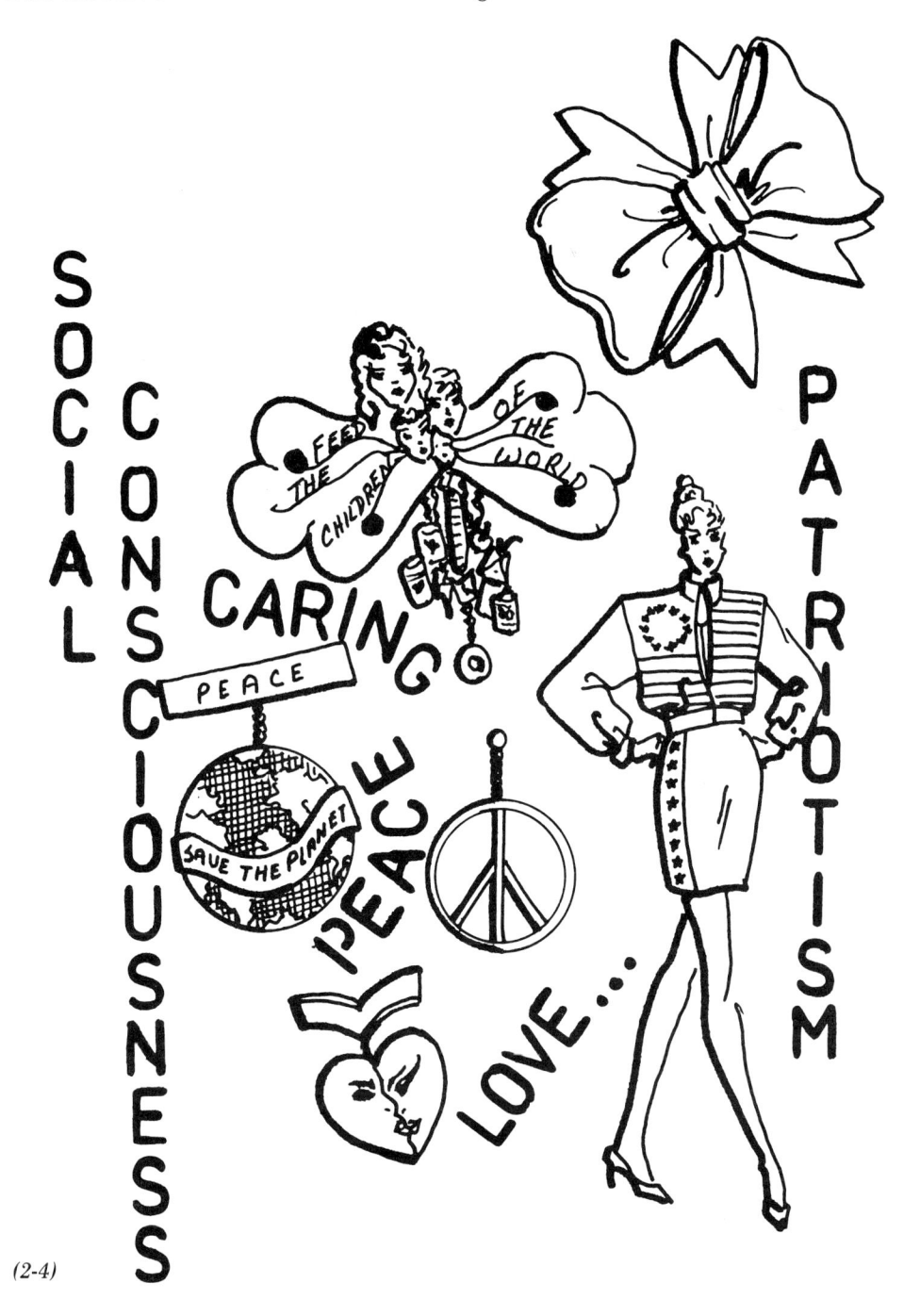

PSYCHOLOGY OF FASHION: Realizing Your Innate Desires 29

(2-4)

In some cases, an idea will just arise, and a select few will expound on it. Sometimes, the idea will catch on in a big way and become a major fashion phenomenon. You may recall *Out of Africa*, a movie that played a major role in fashion prints, colors, and silhouettes. After its release in 1985, there were many animal prints mixed with ethnic African prints and motifs. There was also an indulgence in fur, feathers, netting, and tortoise shell. Colors were influenced by that film. Khakis, grays, olives, and taupes were everywhere. Finally, there was an influx of hats, safari jackets, and jodphurs. By keeping yourself in tune with what is going on in the world, you can stay one step ahead of the game. If you feel that your wardrobe cannot withstand too many novelty items, use accessories that pick up on current trends to keep you with the times. It is not necessary to fill your closet with things that may be overnight trends or fads. Just get a couple of pieces, here and there, to give you and your closet a lift.

Although silhouette is third on the scale of importance (in most people's minds), it is a very crucial factor. A wonderful color and print does not ensure the silhouette is for you. The fact that a garment looks hideous on a hanger does not mean it lacks the potential of being a knockout on the body.

Once again, forecasters play a role in determining guidelines for the next season's hottest looks. If fashion designers predict short skirts, you'd better believe you will be wearing a shorter skirt. If the following year longer skirts are predicted, you will be buying longer skirts. If they are confused about what length to predict, you will probably be wearing pants. The next year split skirts will be the rage. The following year will probably bring city shorts. And so the story goes...

Thank goodness for fashion innovators that have the fortitude to take the reins. If the design is good enough, the rest of the industry will try to grab the coattails. New York fashion designer, Donna Karan, presented just such a phenomenon with her Scuba Suit. Pretty soon, everyone was doing it: dresses with zippers, suits with zippers; tight pants, tight skirts, fitted jackets; and

PSYCHOLOGY OF FASHION: Realizing Your Innate Desires

even shoes with zippers. Who knows where the idea came from. Perhaps she was on vacation and went scuba diving. She realized the potential for a comfortable, sophisticated, and figure flattering silhouette. Maybe, it was just a design she came up with. Still, the inspiration had to come from somewhere, and only Donna Karan knows where.

Mega-star Madonna can be thanked for the evolution of innerwear to outerwear. It was Madonna's fame that really brought it to the street level. Adoring fans wanted to imitate the desperately sought-after idol. Designers focused the trend towards their own needs. Subsequently, an explosion of bustiers, bodysuits, bra-tops, crinolines, and merriwidow sportswear erupted. Now, at the couture level, these trends are emerging in evening attire. It is lingerie - inspired eveningwear, from slip dresses to bodysuits. Madonna made it happen.

War touches fashion in a way that many people do not even realize. World War I influenced styles of the period in a number of ways. The most obvious was the move into more comfortable, practical clothing. Such apparel was required for participation in many jobs and outside roles women had taken over from men. Skirts were shortened to several inches above the ankle and widened around the hem. Prior to war, the fashion was the hobble skirt. Aside from being very long, this skirt was impossible for women to wear if they were engaged in any chore requiring a lot of movement. Also because of the war, certain fabrications had to be replaced due to lack of availability. Colors lightened, due to the lack of chemicals used for dyestuff.

World War II confirmed these allegations of change. Once again, certain fabrications were scarce. Hemlines shortened even further, and women began wearing trousers. Pants were easier to work in.

The latest Gulf Crisis of 1990 between Iraq and Allied Forces, once again, proved the point. Prior to the Gulf War, hemlines were long. Holiday 1990 and Spring 1991 brought an influx of short skirts, hot pants, and skin-baring garments. Vietnam influenced the fashions of the 1960's in the same manner, producing a melange of hot pants, micro-minis, and catsuits. Designers become more extravagant in styling to take people's minds off the present situation. Hemlines go up because men are away, women go to work, and women desire to feel sexy when loved ones are not with them. Some fashion experts may say it is just coincidence. Well, this coincidence is very much on target.

All of the silhouettes that emerge on the fashion scene will not be for you. You must understand your body, its flaws, and its fine points. If the style does not suit you, the color or print will be of no consequence. Silhouette is not only dependent on the design of the garment or your figure, but also the fabric of which it consists. A garment in silk will hang completely differently from a garment in wool or linen. Later in the book, you will learn how to steer clear of these barriers. As far as silhouette, fashion is a recurring cycle. If you keep something long enough, it will come back in style.

3 COLOR-PHOBIA:
Overcoming The Fear Of Color

— What do I do when "my" colors are not in style? Buy a new wardrobe?

— I have been color-coded and cannot wear any color unless it matches my swatches.

— Do I wear pink, red, or peach lipstick with this oufit?

— Can I mix wool and ultra-suede?

— Who wants to buy anything in polyester?

The most surprising thing about color is the fact that people fear it. It is like the crystal figurine that is not to be touched. If it falls, it could shatter. NEWS FLASH: Color shatters beautifully! Color surrounds us completely. Yet, we are greatly intimidated by it. We tend to make the mixture of color more complicated than it is. There is no wrong combo. Every color is beautiful with every other color. Vivid hints are right before our eyes.

Look to nature for reassurances. Autumn is a flourish of leaves in glorious color: red, mustard, burnt orange, and burgundy. Sometimes all of these colors exist in a singular leaf.

Summertime sunsets are a garnished spectrum of pinks, peaches, purples, and navys. In the course of one sunset, a symphony of color is orchestrated.

Fire heats up with crackling orange flames, burning red wisps, and burnt brown edges. Mother nature's natural pigmentation is a complimentary lesson in color companionship. The entity of color has no barriers. People construct the barriers. Cohabitation of color is as natural as living and breathing. Our Creator's beauty was not expressed in a single color. His creation would be lacking in beauty, if not embellished with the magnificence of shade, hue, and intensity. Each pigment complements the other.

To become comfortable with color, you must "feel" it, "smell" it, "hear" it, and "taste" it. You must "become" color. If you are "Red," you will feel hot, smell like cinnamon, have a deep throaty voice, and taste like cherries. As "Red" looking for companionship, you must see who you are attracted to:

Senses	Black	White	Yellow
Feels	Cold	Clean	Like Sunshine
Smells Like	Sophistication	Freshness	Citrus
Sounds Like	Silence	A Whisper	Laughter
Tastes Like	Blackberries	Crushed Ice	Lemon

COLOR-PHOBIA: Overcoming The Fear Of Color

Senses	Blue	Green	Purple
Feels	Soft	Woodsy	Velvety
Smells Like	The Wind	Peppermint	Potpourri
Sounds Like	Moaning	Loving Voices	Rain
Tastes Like	Cotton Candy	Kiwi Fruit	Grape Soda

You could blend with any of them. The next week, you may want to find some new companions.

After experiencing the ecstasy of each color's character, you must meet its family. Every color encompasses an enormous family. There are hundreds of shades lighter and darker than the original. The more you see color, the more comfortable you become. Also, seeing an array of pigments and their various shades stimulates color coordination. The primary reason fashion people are so well versed at mixing color is their constant exposure to it. Allow your color consciousness to expand. Open your eyes to color. Open your mind to color. Let your hands experience COLOR.

Columns "A" through "H" are families of primary and secondary colors. Notice the expanse of color range within a color family. Furthermore, these are only seven variations of each color selection. There are hundreds of additional shades between and beyond our illustrated examples. Please Note: The following concepts will be discussed in more detail in the following chapter.

Beautiful wardrobe combinations can be made through a single color family. The existing expanse of a color, from lightest to darkest is, indeed, varied. Most people are not even aware that certain colors are related. Did you know that ice pink and rust are both from the red family? Did you know that fuchsia and plum are cousins? The next three examples clearly illustrate the numerous wardrobing options existing within our closets.

36 EUROFASHION: Unleashing The Designer In You

(3-1) A B C D

COLOR-PHOBIA: Overcoming The Fear Of Color 37

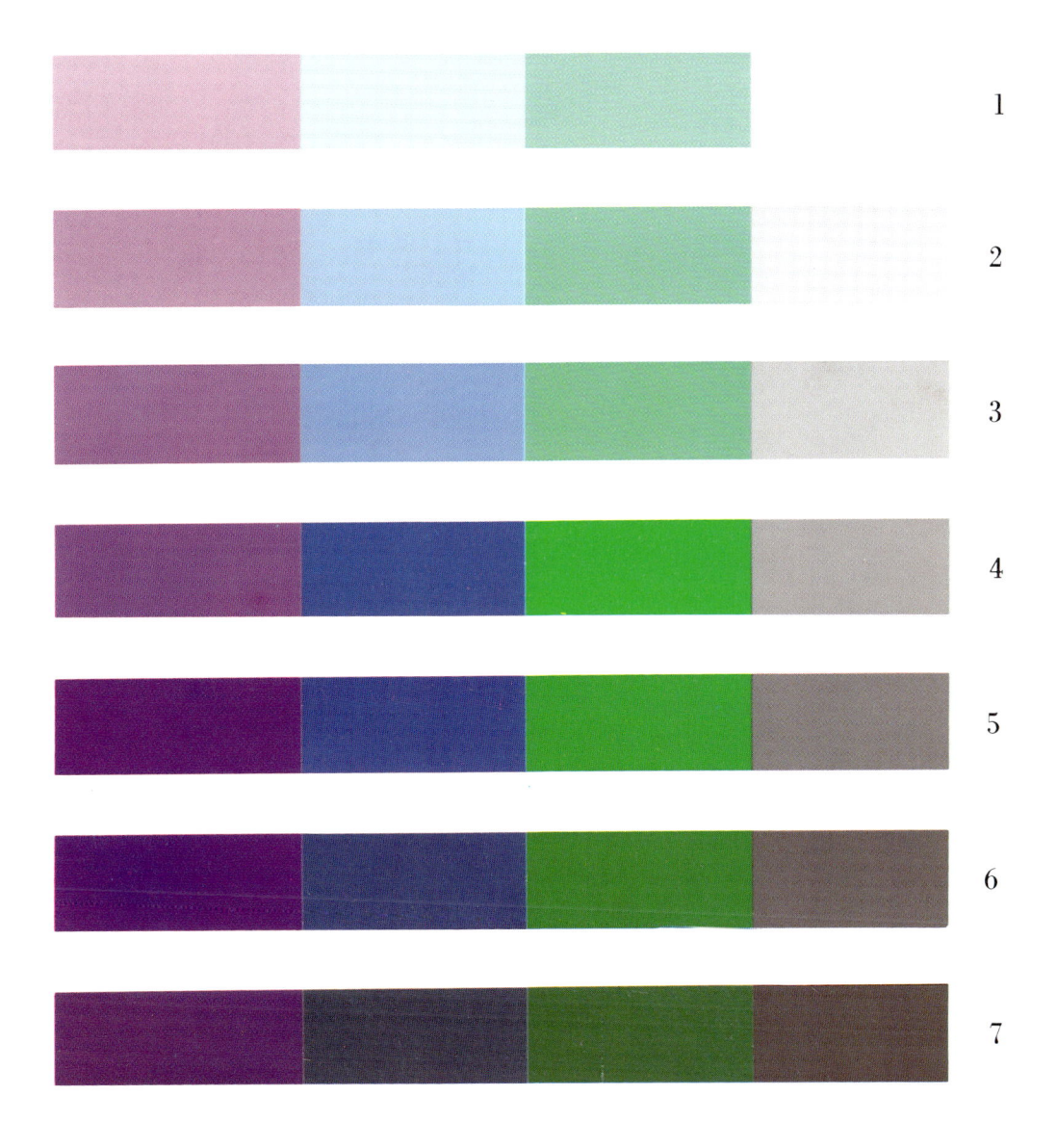

1
2
3
4
5
6
7

(3-2)   E   F   G   H

38   EUROFASHION: Unleashing The Designer In You

Column "A" ---

   Did you ever realize that lemon would lead to olive? Wouldn't that be a pretty combination? Add canary to that combo. Visualize "A1," "A4," and "A7" in an ensemble. (Fig. 3-3)

(3-3)

COLOR-PHOBIA: Overcoming The Fear Of Color 39

(3-4)

Column "B" ---

Orange begins as peach and ends as rust. Contemplate a combo of "B3," "B4," and "B7." (Fig. 3-4)

40   EUROFASHION: Unleashing The Designer In You

Column "H" ---

   Have you ever wondered why black and white make such a striking combination? They are from the same family. Gray lightens to white and darkens to black. A conglomeration of gray shades is a complement to family togetherness. (Fig. 3-5)

(3-5)

COLOR-PHOBIA: Overcoming The Fear Of Color 41

(3-6)

Next, span the spectrum of color existing within each horizontal row. Don't these colors look pretty together? Each horizontal row contains colors of equal intensity. Row 1 is reminiscent of Easter eggs and pretty floral dresses. Row 4 exhilarates the system. Thoughts of colored confetti and carnivals prance through the mind. Row 6 educes a feeling of serene regality, sophistication,

42   EUROFASHION: Unleashing The Designer In You

and the finer things in life. Any of these collaborations present beautiful contrast combinations. Take a peek.

Row 1, Selections "E" "G" "H" (Fig. 3-6)

The use of lighter shades does not restrict images of fun, classic, sophisticated, or funky. Imagery is all according to what you want.

Row 5, Selections "A" "B" "C" (Fig. 3-7)

A cornucopia of autumn tints abounds, from sedate to sassy.

(3-7)

COLOR-PHOBIA: Overcoming The Fear Of Color 43

(3-8)

Row 6, Selections "A" "C" "D" "E" (Fig. 3-8)
An intensity of color allows you the option of wearing colors you may not like on yourself. The key is to accent the ensemble with your good colors. Place one of your good colors near your face. In this case, the model's better colors were fuchsia and purple.

If we can mix colors of the same family, and we can mix assorted colors of the same intensity, what else is there??? The whole world is there...CROSS, COLLABORATE, and CREATE!!!

You can mix pastels, brights, muteds, and darks. It is another form of contrast mixing. As we said in the beginning, every color blends beautifully with every other color. Although this is a more fashion-forward method of dressing, it is all around us. The next time you get on the highway, take a moment to dissect your surroundings. The road is a charcoal gray with a mustard yellow striping. The trees and grass are a medium to dark green. Finally, the sky is light blue. In this scenario are a pastel, a muted, a bright, and a dark. We view this image daily and we never question the combination of color. In addition, we see houses of pink, beige, blue...more and more color combinations; and we don't know what colors go together? Mix it all. The odder the combo, the more eyecatching the appearance.

COLOR-PHOBIA: Overcoming The Fear Of Color 45

Combo "G7" "C3" "A4" (Fig. 3-9)

(3-9)

46 EUROFASHION: Unleashing The Designer In You

Combo "F5" "E3" "H4" (Fig. 3-10)

(3-10)

COLOR-PHOBIA: Overcoming The Fear Of Color 47

Combo "B2" "C6" "D4" (Fig. 3-11)

(3-11)

There was a time when people wanted to match emerald with emerald. That time has passed. It is still acceptable. But, don't you want more? When teaching someone about color, we ask them to name colors they believe would be hideous together. Then, we prove them wrong. In our mind, all colors were conceived to harmonize with each other. There is no ugly combination. You must overcome your fear, in order to forge ahead into EUROFASHION.

Everyone knows which colors look good on him/her and which ones do not. You know what shades make you feel good about yourself. How do you enjoy wearing the rest of the colors? Some consumers do find difficulty shopping when "their" colors are not as evident in the stores. However, you should not be one of those consumers. You should enjoy every phase of fashion. Color is one of the most exciting areas of fashion with which to experiment. Put things to your advantage. Wear all colors. For those colors you find unflattering, change your makeup, or allow accessories to assist you in making those colors wearable.

Cosmetic industry trends follow a parallel course to current clothing color trends. A qualified cosmetologist can guide you in blending your various "right" colors. She can also show you how to take the peach lipstick you are not supposed to wear and blend it with the pink lipstick you do wear. These new blends can set off your skin tone and your ensemble. Times have changed drastically in all areas of fashion, including cosmetics. You do not have to think twice about mixing pinks/reds/oranges/peaches or blues/greens/purples/olives. The most difficult step is trying. See the total look. Not just a face...Not just the outfit...See the entire, total look.

Wigs and hair pieces encompass another area that allows you to alter your appearance to suit a color or vice versa. High fashion models in the 1990's, like Naomi Campbell, have provided authorization for the commencement of a new trend. You may wear a different hair color with every ensemble: blond, red, platinum, lime, banana, or black. With different hair colors, you can take on different moods, and your skin can achieve variations in tone. Furthermore, your expanse of wearable colors increases and your cosmetic options are insurmountable.

For those people who would never have the nerve to try wigs nor the initiative to change their makeup, there are alternative solutions. Accessories are an easy solution and first step towards change. Accessories are to women what dogs are to men: best friends. Scarves can be a great deal of assistance. There are many methods of tying and using them. Scarves also encompass a variety of color. If you are wearing an unflattering color near your face, add a scarf of a flattering color at the neck. It is that easy. You can even create new color combinations and new fashion.

Jewelry is another simple method of changing the color at your face. A choker will act as a separation block. Gold, silver, and copper are nice complements to almost any color. A longer chain can pull out the colors you wish to accent. Chains in multicolor are just as effective as monotone pieces.

Pins are an artistic resource. They are also one of the best image makers. Aside from super color selections, a variety of looks exists within this accessory group. You can appear conservative, high-fashion, comfortable, or funky.

Finally, an assortment of different accessory items can create exciting looks and complements of color. Accessories are a simple, interesting way to begin your journey through wardrobing.

After feeling relaxed about color, you need to get acquainted with what you will wear. Clothing fabrications come in all weights, types, and thicknesses. It is important for you to know what fabrications will work well together.

People are always wary of combining different fabrications. Perhaps in the past, certain fabric combinations were considered improper. However, times have changed. Everything is possible. Create your own looks. Designers continuously experiment in new fabric combinations. Only through experimentation are acceptable mixtures unearthed. The many variations of appearance that one fabric may have also enhance fusion opportunities. Numerous new treatments unfolding in the marketplace assist our quest of wardrobing feats:

sueding, sandwashing, stonewashing, sun drying, thermal sensing, embossing, puff printing, or melanging.

At one time, polyester was classified as a raunchy fabric detested by most. Now, you can find gorgeous polyesters with the look and the feel of silk. Polyesters were always associated with the double-knits Grandma used to wear. Today, polyester knits retain hands of suede, cashmere, and cotton. Many eveningwear fabrics, such as some taffetas, georgettes, chiffons, crepes, and satins, contain polyester. Polyester is the most versatile fabrication to choose from. Furthermore, it requires the easiest care.

The luxury of silk has fallen within our grasp because of new washing properties. There is also a wider range of silk fabrications available. Many ways to alter the hand and appearance exist. Sueded silk has a velvety hand and elegant luster. Washed silk tends to be sportier and retains a dulled look. These are just a couple of examples from a list of many.

Denim is another fabric that is available as thin as handerchief linen, as thick as burlap, and varying densities between the two extremes. Denim has been stonewashed, studded, sandwashed, spliced, sun dried, jewelled, and zippered.

The development of new treatments and fabrications has increased the length of seasonal wear. Fashion is becoming seasonless. Suede used to be for winter. Linen used to be for spring and summer. Dark colors were worn from August to January. Light colors were worn from January to July. Now, you can find suede in spring and summer footwear collections. Sportswear and eveningwear companies are offering varied weights of linen throughout the year. This new plan is beneficial to wardrobing. It creates longevity for the wear of many garments. New blending opportunities for fabric are also expressible. If you are apprehensive of trying new combinations, go into the stores and see what is being shown. You will come across displays illustrating many fabric combos. You will even find some garments that are a coalition of many fabrics: silk, wool, leather, and lace. Sculptured and patchwork designs are an artist's

COLOR-PHOBIA: Overcoming The Fear Of Color

masterpiece where fabric is the medium. Your wardrobe is putty in the hands. Mold it into one-of-a-kind works of art. Mix whatever you want. If you feel good in it nothing else matters. It is your closet, your imagination, and you. YOU can mix:

"You Can Mix"	Example
Fabrics That Are The Same	Wool/Wool
Fabrics of the Same Density	Cashmere/Silk Tussah
Fabrics of Different Density	Mohair/Lame'
Fabrics of Different Weights	Leather/Lace
Soft and Hard Fabrics	Silk/Linen
Opaque and Sheer Fabrics	Denim/Chiffon
Lusterful and Bisque Fabrics	Satin/Batiste
Knits and Wovens	Interlocks/Gabardine
Prints and Woven Patterns	Floral/Woven Houndstooth
Animate and the Inanimate	Flowers/Any Fabric

The transcedence into cocktail "sportswear" is evidence that any combination is possible. An example of cocktail sportswear might consist of sequin overlayed silk camisoles under sweater cardigans and organza bottoms. Wool jersey turtlenecks and floor length silk taffeta skirts are another popular combo. Lace is very prominent, when adorned with leather and beading.

Sportswear has been altered dramatically. Poplin city shorts and a bomber jacket are likely to have a gold lame' tee shirt. Rayon separates are accented with lace embellishments. Linen, silk, and wool jackets are encrusted with rhinestones on lapels, pockets, and front torsos. Excitingly, all of these are for casual elegance during the DAY!!!

You could say fashions are becoming dressier. You could say designers are dressing down fabrications to make them more available to a larger consumer audience. If designers are not limiting their collections, why should you limit your closet? If you buy a three-piece suit, consider each piece a separate entity. Otherwise, you trap yourself into wearing it only one way. When you view your clothes as separates, you expand your wardrobe. The smallest wardrobe can seem like a clothing store if each piece is utilized to its fullest potential. By limiting yourself, you are unable to experience the fun of fashion. And...FASHION SHOULD BE FUN!

4 FUTURE LIFE EXPECTANCY:
Unearthing Creativity

— I have nice clothing. What do I do with it?

— How do I know which scarf will appear dressier?

— How do they mix those prints and carry it off?

— It all looks so easy until I start trying.

Having an understanding of the conception and birth of a garment, you can make sure your clothing has a full and productive life. Many of us do not realize the full extent of a wardrobe's capabilities.

When most people shop for clothing, they limit their options because of lack of exposure to new and fashion-forward trends. For example, most shoppers purchase solid scarves for print ensembles and print scarves for their solid ensembles. Not only are they limiting their scarves, but also the garments for which they purchased the scarves. When dealing with a print selection, you may retain two points of view: **minimal focus** or **maximal focus**. Minimal focus is the method in which you can focus on the colors that are most minutely presented. Maximal focus is the method in which you focus on the color that covers the most area. For example, view the two models on the next page (Fig. 4-1). The model has on a tangerine dress that needs to be accessorized. She has two basic options for the outfits, the minimal and maximal focus techniques. The accessory decision has been narrowed down to the two scarves illustrated. The first scarf is miniature paisley and has very little of the tangerine in it (minimal focus). The second scarf is floral and has splashes of tangerine throughout (maximal focus). Both scarves look good. However, the use of each scarf depicts the ensemble from a different perspective. In this particular case, the maximal focus projects a more sophisticated appearance. The minimal focus projects a more playful, active mood. This is not to say maximal is always sophisticated and minimal is always active. It really changes with each situation. Take a look at Figure 4-2 for further depiction of these two techniques (using garment mixture).

FUTURE LIFE EXPECTANCY: Unearthing Creativity 55

(4-1)

In this scenario, the model is looking for a blouse to match the floral suit. Her first attempt is a chocolate blouse (minimal focus). The second selection is a sand blouse (maximal focus). In this case, the minimal focus technique resulted in the dressier look. The colors you select, the ensemble involved, and the way you put yourself together create the final mood. These are the moments

(4-2)

when you can play the role of designer. You should not limit yourself from trying new things and diversifying from what you consider the norm. Aside from print-to-solid and solid-to-print combinations, there are other alternatives to such puzzling situations. A second alternative available to shoppers is the use of solid scarves, contrast or tonal, on solid garments. To assist in the selection of a solid scarf for a solid outfit, you can go back to Chapter 3. As you learned in that chapter, the color choice is entirely up to you. You may stay within a particular color family or color intensity, or you may choose colors at random.

The third option concerns the use of print scarves for print ensembles. Print on print options will be discussed in detail, later in this chapter.

American and European designers pave our education before us. We need to look ahead and follow their path. By watching their combinations of color and compilations of prints, we can upgrade our level of dressing. Once we are comfortable with these changes, our new outlook can seep into other areas of our wardrobes and daily lives. Not many people can afford the lifestyle of purchasing from a couturier, but that limitation does not mean we cannot assimilate some of their wonderful ideas.

There are many new methods of dressing. New ways of changing and creating from an existing wardrobe are emerging. As another alternative, you may wish to change your image through new purchases. In the course of the next few pages, I will introduce four methods of clothing collaboration that will enable you to become more at ease in mixing scarves, other accessories, garments in your wardrobe, and future purchases. The four methods of dressing discussed are "Tonal," "Contrast," "Print Collaboration," and "Print Mixing."

Tonal dressing is the method in which all articles relate in color. A color is broken down among the different shades in which it is available. Then, each article of the ensemble falls within that color family. Tonal dressing can be achieved through the use of one color throughout or, as stated above, variations of a color distributed within an ensemble.

Contrast dressing is the method in which a mood is achieved through the use of a sharp contrast or break within an ensemble. Contrast dressing can be attained through a single color break or a multiple color break. It is most successful when using colors totally unrelated to the base garment. In this method of dressing, the use of muted tones is as striking as the use of brights.

Print collaboration is the method in which two or more prints of related coloration or pattern are combined within an ensemble. By selecting items that possess two or more common colors, outfits are "blended" together to project images of Eurodressing and high style.

Print mixing is the method in which two or more prints of totally unrelated coloration or pattern are combined. This type of mixing can be categorized as high fashion and is usually the most difficult to comprehend and carry through.

Now that you have a definitive understanding of the four concepts, you need to study visual explanations. Models will assist us. We have chosen three outfits for each concept. The outfits chosen are of a somewhat tailored nature. However, once you have grasped an understanding, you can adapt these methods to any area of your wardrobe. As you go through the examples, watch the ways in which color is used. Realize that color is nothing to be afraid of. Combining color is a very easy process. Becoming comfortable with prints will follow your acceptance of color. You need to allow yourself to experiment a few times so that use of color becomes "old hat." Kenu, our model, will assist in illustrating the wardrobe concepts.

"Tonal Dressing" -- the method in which an ensemble is put together
using one or more variations of a single color family.

Kenu's first three outfits are examples of tonal dressing, starting with the least complicated form. The first suit illustrates the use of a solid color from head to toe. There is a misconception that a break in a garment is required somewhere. That is a fallacy. You can see for yourself that this is a very elegant, sophisticated, and simple display of the female form. Silhouette and color are

FUTURE LIFE EXPECTANCY: Unearthing Creativity

the focal points when wearing an ensemble in this manner. Be sure both points are well thought out. Usually, any color is lovely when worn solid. If this style of dress is just too plain for you, you may try a tonal variation, as illustrated on the following two models in Figure 4-3.

(4-3)

Model 2 illustrates the richness of tonal dressing through the use of muted shades. To capture the essence of this style of dressing, you begin with a single color choice. We decided to work with the family of browns. Then, you must select a second shade, lighter or darker but within the family, to designate the tone and mood you are trying to relay. With this direction, you are free to complete your ensemble with one, two, ten, or one hundred additional colors (still remaining within your chosen family of colors). We began with taupe and chocolate. Then we added a medium tone, mocha. You may wish to combine two very light shades with a very dark one. Perhaps, you would like the collaboration of four very light shades. The choice is completely yours. **Nothing is wrong.**

Model 3 illustrates the dramatics of tonal dressing in its most extravagant sense. In this example, we have allowed you sight of the extreme. Kenu grasps the farthest corners of the spectrum, while staying within the limits of one color family. If you look at a rainbow, you will see that the colors run together. The same idea follows through. In a family of reds, you will find orange-reds and pink-reds. The choices of color are endless. It is up to the expanse of your imagination and the boldness of your personality. The combination of burgundy, tomato red, and hot pink may seem shocking to you. This one, however, is a "hot" look that will bring a rush of compliments and approving nods. Not only will you establish yourself as a fashion plate, but you will also leave behind a trail of people that will show up later in a similar ensemble. Other combinations you may wish to experiment in are royal/purple/turquoise, lemon/mustard/olive, or white/gray/black. The options are endless. This form of dressing will allow you to blend into the crowd or be the focus of it; whichever you prefer. Tonal dressing will also expand your wardrobe. Old suits will become new. Now you are ready to conquer "Contrast Dressing."

> "Contrast Dressing" --- the method in which an ensemble is put together using two or more colors (of the same or different intensities) belonging to different color families.

FUTURE LIFE EXPECTANCY: Unearthing Creativity

Kenu's next three outfits are examples of contrast dressing. Although it may appear overpowering at first glance, it is a very simple and easy way of dressing. You may recall seeing unit priced combinations, such as these, sold in stores. Spring/Summer 1989 introduced many contrast looks into the retail market; 1990 followed with a much heavier play on contrast dressing, implementing sportswear. Here you can see the use of contrast dressing, from its most conservative aspect to its most outstanding. The first outfit engages the subtlety of accessories to express a simplistic individuality. Sometimes, one odd color added to an otherwise sedate combination can become the perfect "pop" necessary to set you apart from the rest. "Pop" is not only achieved through the addition of brights, but also through the use of muted tones. Your main obstacle is to conquer your timidity of combining and creating unique color palettes of your own. Let's take a look. (Fig. 4-4)

Outfit number one is a tangerine two-piece. Rather than using the normal navy, black, or bone, we decided to try something with a twist. The bright yellow is the perfect "pop." She could have easily worn a third bright color at the feet. Yet, we opted for the more toned down look.

The second outfit delves deeper into the beauty of contrasting. Kenu has begun experimenting with articles of clothing, as well as accessories. There is no end to the expanse of a wardrobe, once each piece is properly utilized. This outfit also displays the use of muted tones in contrast.

We specifically chose a two-tone jacket for this example. Many people feel limited in the use of any two-tone item. It is very easy to create new outfits without ever using either of the colors involved. Here, we have chosen colors of the same intensity and put them together. The peach and banana work beautifully with the turquoise and gray. Consequently, you are not limited in your degree of substitution where contrasting is concerned.

The final ensemble is a wonderful exploitation of color which exudes taste, style, and pizazz. Each item is of a different color and complements all other articles involved. Again, you can see that you are not limited to the colors in the jacket. Your goal should be to remain in the same intensity. Once you have accomplished this degree of mixing, you can move into mixing colors of varying intensities and color families. Chapter 3 does venture into that area and provides illustrations.

(4-4)

FUTURE LIFE EXPECTANCY: Unearthing Creativity

Now that you are feeling a little more comfortable about mixing colors, it is time to delve into the mixture of prints. This is an area at which you will have to work a little harder. Most fashion consumers do not adapt easily to this concept; it has to grow on you with time. For the average person that does not deal with fashion on a day to day basis, print mixing may seem a little insane. But, wait until you see!!! It is a whole other world, and it is an exciting one. Once you understand how it works, you will become frustrated at more simple combinations. You will start treading further on the path of "Eurofashion." Study the next few combinations very carefully. Upon completion of this section, please put the book away for a few hours. Then, come back and study the illustrations again. You may have to do this a few times to gain comprehension of this alien concept. But, as you walk through the stores, you will find yourself putting together odd combinations and prints. What will emerge is a wonderful new wardrobe and a fantastic new image. You will recognize a new self-confidence about yourself, and others will notice also.

"Print Collaboration" --- the method in which two or more prints
of related coloration or pattern are combined within a single ensemble.

There is a basic principle to the "print on print" concept: a relation of coloration or print must exist so that the eye has a line to follow and consolidate as a total entity. In simple terms, either the print needs to be repeated, or two or more colors need to be repeated. Let us begin with the "Positive/Negative" styling concept.

"Positive/Negative" refers to the redundance of a print in a directly opposite combination than the base print. Variations on this concept can be achieved through print size changes and uses of the same color but different print. Model 1, Figure 4-5, is an illustration of dots in black and white used in the positive/negative manner. The blouse we have chosen is white with black dots. To achieve our goal, we located a scarf of the exact same print. The only difference was the scarf's reversal of color allocation.

A broader use of positive/negative is presented in Kenu's second ensemble.

64   EUROFASHION: Unleashing The Designer In You

An entire garment is used to relay this image. The scarf and pant are of one print; the top is in a correlating print of proper proportion. The reason this outfit works is simply the restriction of all pieces having the same coloration. The checkered cummerbund adds an extra spark and finishing touch.

(4-5)

FUTURE LIFE EXPECTANCY: Unearthing Creativity   65

Model 3 illustrates the thoughts of a designer in his or her projection of utilizing many prints in one ensemble. Through a conglomeration of related geometric prints placed together in collage formations within each article of clothing, the image portraying fashion expertise is allotted to the wearer. In this case, the jacket and skirt were purchased together. We wanted to add another piece to the outfit to create a layered look. However, we did not want to use a solid. We found a fifth print, using the same colors, in a v-neck blouse. If we had not mentioned our putting this ensemble together, you would have kept on believing it came as a three piece. We hope this illustration lifts any timidity about trying some odd combinations.

The second level of print collaboration places emphasis on your ability to mix color. When browsing through stores, you may see articles of clothing by different designers using the same print in different colorations. Try combining the different colorations in one outfit. It is a very fresh new approach to dressing that has not been explored in too much depth. It is your chance to shine, through the cultivation of this new technique. Figure 4-6 shows how accessories can be used to carry out this concept. Model 1 illustrates the use of a scarf of the same print as the dress. However, the colors are different. This accomplishment is really quite simple. Imagine the prints as solids. Any colors you feel comfortable mixing as solid components will mix beautifully as uniform prints. Kenu's first outfit was done in a pink/purple combination to show colorations that are more common. Once you feel comfortable with colors that you know, you will feel more adept at mixing up new combos.

Kenu's second outfit gives a little insight into unique color mixtures. We also wanted you to see how easy it is to venture away from colors of a two-tone suit. The suit sets off the two print colors and vice versa. First, we decided what color we would like to see with the green suit. The choice was turquoise, since it is a newer fashion forward look. We also wanted something that would catch attention. The next decision was what scarf to use. It was important to find a color of the same intensity to achieve the dressier look desired. We

66   EUROFASHION: Unleashing The Designer In You

also needed a color that would complement the other two. Purple was the eye-catching color choice. Purple looks pretty with both green and turquoise. Through the process of elimination, we decided. As you can see, this outfit looks as if it came right from a New York fashion house. Wear what is com-

(4-6)

fortable; and, on occasion, do not feel afraid to take chances. Soon after, taking the risk will become a habit.

Model 3 is an explosion of print and color. Through the use of the same print, the beauty of color is allowed to shine through. Although each piece is a different color, a unity exists because of the print. As we said before, the mixed print concepts are not for everyone and many people cannot reason the thinking behind them. You have to be yourself and wear what makes you feel comfortable. These ideas take a little longer to grow on some people than on others. Once you adapt, you will find your neighbors copying you.

The third area of print collaboration involves the mixture of prints where there are two or more related colors. For example, try a stripe consisting of purple, magenta, and emerald mixed with a floral of the same colors; or perhaps, envision a floral with red, blue, green, and orange mixed with a paisley of red, purple, and yellow. We know these ideas may be difficult to visualize, but they are beautiful combinations and such a mixture is very simple, once you gain proper understanding.

The next pages provide you many visual aids focusing on this area of discussion. (Figures 4-7 and 4-8) Model 1 is the simplest of all the sketches shown. The solid jacket and blouse accent the rosebud skirt very well. However, the addition of the wide-striped scarf really adds the "zing" necessary to set the outfit apart from the ordinary. It is a new touch that requires thought on proportions, colors, and image making. In determining what type of print goes with what, first look at your colors and decide what you consider important. Secondly, decide what kind of print you want: casual, career, elegant. Finally, decide what prints match proportionately to the print you are mixing. The color combination, in addition to the fabric and print, completes whatever look you are trying to portray. This imagery is the understated method of being "chic-ly" in fashion.

The first item on Model 1 was the floral skirt. We wanted to select two colors that would coincide with the dominant colors in the floral. We selected

68 EUROFASHION: Unleashing The Designer In You

(4-7)

FUTURE LIFE EXPECTANCY: Unearthing Creativity 69

the base color, mustard, for the blazer. This choice would allow for a smooth continuation of color. For a rich contrast, we selected the wine for the camisole. There were many choices of prints that would mix with florals: plaids/florals, stripes/florals, dots/florals, paisley/florals, checks/florals. We desired a career look. The decision would be between checks, stripes, and plaids. We went with stripes. We wanted a stripe that contained only the colors of the floral pattern. The end result is a very classy, understated, career look. All we have done is color-by-number. The colors were given. We only had to select the proper numbers and placements.

Model 2 has elements of a contrast mixture. The revival of the sixties brought back bright colors, odd combinations, and psychedelic prints. We have used the inspiration of the sixties to better illustrate the methods involved. The top and pant are of totally unrelated colors. Still, they look as if they belong together. In the sixties, items such as these were worn without accessories to pull the colors together. This would have been worn with the addition of a great pair of earrings, a belt, and a "groovy" pair of shoes. However, some people feel the prints do not match unless pulled together in some way. And, to successfully illustrate print collaboration, we need a tie-in for both pieces.

Kenu happened to have a scarf of these colors. The ensemble looks great either way. Another point we would like to express concerns the execution of fashion trends. Kenu did not purchse these items together. The red and orange pant has a red and orange top to go with it. The turquoise and yellow stripe top has a matching mini. New outfits do exist within your own wardrobe; your wardrobe and imagination just need to be tested.

The third model takes print collaboration one step further. Here are two prints that have only a couple of similar colors. Also, the intervention of color blocking complicates understanding. We began with a camisole and a pair of city shorts. The print on these two pieces was a combination check and floral. Kenu happened to have this wonderful color blocked jacket in her wardrobe. It would fit perfectly with the look we were trying to achieve, casual elegance. But how do you make it match? The main reason the jacket worked so well with the short set is the existence of touches of olive and royal in both items. Still, something was missing that would pull the whole ensemble together. We decided to look for a scarf. Since we already had a check and a floral, we decided to go with dots. We knew to look for a scarf that had characteristics of both items. We came up with a matching polka dot scarf and socks. The scarf had the turquoise and royal of the short set. It also had the exact colors of the jacket, with the exception of the olive. We had attained our goal of casual elegance and found it in a one-of-a-kind ensemble.

Model 1, in Figure 4-8, is an outfit that we put together. You must admit that it looks as if it were bought that way. We wanted you to get a really good look at what items of apparel, more than likely, exist in your closet. You are a fashion plate and do not even realize it. The awareness of the capabilities you possess begins by your opening your closet doors. This outfit shows matching, color for color. Most people decide what colors they like and usually end up with a closet full of those shades. The ironic thing is that most people do not even realize what kind of mixtures exists within the realm of their closet. The point is furthur illustrated on the next two models.

Kenu's closet contained a lot of brown tones. On Model 2, we have tried to illustrate the coalition of two separately purchased outfits. The first outfit consisted of a rust sweater and a printed, full-skirted mini. The colors within the mini were chocolate, rust, red, orange, and cream. The second outfit consisted of a pair of printed leggings and a sweater. The leggings encompassed a color range of chocolate, cream, red, emerald, and purple. The sweater was a melange of all colors represented in the leggings. That some colors were common to both outfits was an instant clue that these two outfits would work well together. The full-skirted mini was placed over the leggings, giving the appearance of a single unit. We decided to tuck the thinner, rust sweater into the mini/legging unit. At the waist, we placed a chocolate belt. Chocolate was chosen for continuity of color. Another focal point was its major content in

FUTURE LIFE EXPECTANCY: Unearthing Creativity 71

(4-8)

both outfits. The final touch was the melange sweater. The colors of the melange sweater picked up the knee-to-ankle border of the leggings to create a fluid line for the eye to follow. The main idea to keep in mind when combining prints is "follow through." Do not allow one area to seem too heavy in a certain color or print. If you have a particular color at the top of an ensemble, and it is weighing down the look or detracting from the look, try repeating the color one or two other places within the ensemble. On the other hand, sometimes people tend to focus too much on one color. The more you work at it, the better your eye will become at focusing on needs.

Kenu's third outfit takes a slightly different approach to print collaboration. We have started with a checked pair of slacks that have a diamond pattern woven on top. We decided to try dissection. We separated the colors of the pants into two categories: top colors and bottom colors. Since the bottom colors are less obvious, we decided to concentrate those colors in the jacket. The top colors were used in the blouse. We found a stripe, eggplant/cinnamon, to offset the diamond pattern. Since the check was more square, we decided to go with the ovality of a floral. These choices of pattern and color were a personal choice to suit Kenu's lifestyle and image. Finally, we chose the peach of the jacket for a cummerbund, because we desired some lightness for an ensemble that was getting too dark for our tastes. Secondly, the light peach was too outstanding and needed to be repeated to subtract from the focus of it. You must make decisions that allow color to work for "you."

> "Print Mixing" --- the method in which two or more prints of totally unrelated coloration or pattern are combined within a single ensemble.

The final category to be discussed is "print mixing." The next three illustrations will provide you some insight into the foreign world of unrelated prints and colorations. The points you must keep in mind to ensure proper execution of this concept are extremely critical: 1-degree of contrast, 2-complement of color, 3-correlation of print sizes, 4-degree of follow through. Now, let us discuss these requirements in detail. Points one through four relate to each other. When analyzing one point, you will venture into the territorial description of another. One point cannot exist without the consideration of the second, third, or fourth and their collaborative result.

Degree of contrast pertains to the way the prints relate to each other. Are the colors too similar, or can each print be seen independently? Do the prints work well together?

Complement of color questions the relationship existing between the colors of the individual prints. Are the colors of print "A" too harsh or the wrong intensity when compared to those of print "B"? Do the colors work well enough together to create the illusion of a purchased coordinated ensemble?

Correlation of print size determines if one print is or is not overpowering of the second. Does a floral get lost with a large check present? Is a mini-dot too miniscule with a miniature paisley? Is there a way to make two oppositely sized prints work together? Is it wrong to place two prints of similar proportion together?

Degree of follow-through interprets the execution of previous questions in relation to the final look of the ensemble. Have we used too much of one particular print? Would the ensemble appear more complete with a repetition of either print? These are the more important of many questions you must ask yourself. Once you truly have a grasp on how to thoroughly execute this concept, confidence will allow you to bypass many of these questions.

The first outfit we will interpret is a checkered dress. In this example (Figure 4-9, Model 1), a scarf is used as a more conservative approach to print mixing. The window-pane check is a 2 x 2 inch print consisting of apple, hunter, aqua, and royal. Black frames each square. The scarf we have selected is a paisley floral of tan, brown, rust, and red. Why did we select this combination of colors? First, we selected colors of the same intensity. Our next focus was to choose colors that would complement each other. To do this, you must look at each color as an individual. Then, determine if it would mix well with each color of the second print. Upon completion of points 1 and 2, we had to select a second print that would not seem too bold or too miniscule with the check. Since the windowpane was bold, we decided to use something smaller in pattern size. Another reason for the smaller print was the intensity of color going on throughout the ensemble. It would have become overpowering with the addition of another bold element.

Kenu's second outfit ventures a little farther. We are trying to build around a paisley suit of cocoa, violet, emerald, and sand. We chose a black and white stripe for the blouse and belt. You will find that stripes, particularly two-toned stripes, will almost always work in print mixing. A black/white stripe or dot has the correct chemistry to create the right effect, regardlesss of the second print or coloration. Usually, a ¼ to ½ inch stripe or dot is a good size for any other print size. You do not even have to think about it. As you see, this outfit has a wonderful crispness and European flair about it. We chose a long sleeve blouse to allow the stripe to show in other areas, rather than just concentrating along the center line of the body. We also used the stripe in the belt to make the waist appear a little longer. The belt also allowed more coverage of the stripe. It is extremely important to follow through in your execution of print mixing. Allowing the print to appear in several other places provides a finished look for the ensemble and provides the onlooker with a line to follow. The purple scarf was used as an accent piece for an extra touch of flair. As a design feature, it has been tucked into the pockets of the skirt.

The final print mix is an eruption of color and pattern. Yet, to the "fashionable" eye, it is an artistic masterpiece. Our palette consisted of a floral, a stripe, and a check. The floral was of red, purple, and orange cabbage roses. The ½ inch stripe consisted of green and white. The check was of hot pink, yellow, red, black, and green. The accessories are up to you. There are ample colors from which to choose. Upon putting this ensemble together, the four critical points were examined. The degree of contrast was perfect. No coloration was too harsh or too sedate. The sizes of each pattern worked very well

FUTURE LIFE EXPECTANCY: Unearthing Creativity

(4-9)

together. Enough area was covered by each print, and the follow-through existed within the check scarf. If you notice carefully, the red from the blouse and the green from the skirt were repeated in the check to allow the eye an association. The final treatment we applied was a black belt to relate to the black in the scarf. Black can sometimes appear heavy. In this situation, it was necessary to place some black elsewhere to lessen the weight of the black in the scarf.

We know this is a lot of material to take in at one time. After the first reading, you may neither feel comfortable with nor understand these innovative ideas. Concepts of fashion are learned processes. You are learning just by looking. The more items you see of this nature, the better chance your brain has to lean toward this way of thinking.

You will need to reread and study this section a few times. Each time you look at the pictures, you will like them a little more. For some, it will require one reading. Others may require one hundred readings. The main thing is not to get discouraged. Seeing and understanding the concepts are your most difficult tasks. Once you accomplish that, the rest is color-by-number. After learning to stay within the lines, you can color anything.

5 A CLOSET CASE:
Birth Of A Wardrobe

— Why couldn't I be 5'10", 115 pounds, and a size 6?

— How could anything possibly look good on this figure?

— Even if I now understand how to mix and match, how do I know what looks good on me?

— Half the things in my closet I don't even wear; what should I do with those?

Now that we have the understanding that fashion has no limitations, we must try to understand our own limitations. The goal is to determine ideas that will be enhancing of better qualities and disguising of weaker areas. Becoming aware of color, fabric, and garment coordination is just the first step in creating a sense of style. Development of a "designer" mind will not be of consequence if you are not happy with yourself or your closet.

All people have things they would like to change about themselves. We have yet to meet a woman satisfied with her appearance. Studies have reported that ninety-six percent of all women are unhappy with their bodies. Size two women have just as many hang-ups as size twenty-two women. Much of this unhappiness is a result of the media idolization of the two percent of "absolutely gorgeous" people that exist. Media exposure catapults a desire to possess "absolutely gorgeous" characteristics. The irony is that the rest of us, ninety-eight percent who fall between plain and very attractive, continue to compare ourselves to the "abolutely gorgeous." Why do we put ourselves down this way? It is an unrealistic measure by which to judge ourselves. The people to whom we should be comparing ourselves are the everyday people we encounter, the "real" people. Furthermore, there should be other attributes which encompass a broader spectrum of our true selves: intelligence, social merit, compassion. When it comes to the judging of beauty, you should just look in the mirror and appreciate the exquisite beauty of what is staring back at you, the Lord's creation. You can be any color, height, size, or shape and be beautiful, if you use the proper accents.

One of the most beautiful women we know is 5'5", and she wears a size twenty. She is more attractive in her clothing than most size four women we have encountered. Furthermore, she receives compliments everywhere she goes, from men and women. A second acquaintance was a beauty queen in her high school days. She is now a size twenty-two and one of the most georgous women inside and out. Aside from being attractive, the beauty both of these women

A CLOSET CASE: Birth Of A Wardrobe

possess is attributed to three important factors: 1-Attitude, 2-Smart Shopping, 3-A Sense of Independence.

Before we get started breaking down the complexities of the three factors, you must understand that every person has problems concerning her figure. We all tend to judge ourselves more harshly than others do. However, such self-criticism is to our benefit. It is the best motivation to work harder towards improved outward appearances.

People love to make excuses for themselves. Having served in retail for more than fifteen years, we have heard them all. Sometimes the excuses are legitimate and sometimes not. "My hips are too wide." "My shoulders are too narrow." "I am swayback." "My neck is too long and thin." "I am too short." "I need to get rid of my stomach." etc... But, the most popular excuse is "I need to lose weight" or "If only I could lose ten more pounds..." Well folks, it is a difficult goal to achieve if it ever happens. We do not mean to burst your bubble but most people are meant to be the way they are. Age has a lot to do with weight gain. The type of job you have also affects weight. Family traits influence much of the way you look. If one of your parents was heavy, you have a chance of being heavy. If you or your mate is petite, there is a strong chance your children will be petite. If you are a big-boned person, no matter what amount of weight you lose, your shoulder width will remain the same. We are not saying you should become nonchalant about your looks. However, do not depreciate yourself or try to accomplish things that are not meant to be. It is better to be your size and healthy than to be ill and still struggling towards the size you wish to be. Do not let anyone fool you. Excessive dieting can damage your system. You could end up with worse problems than when you started.

Why not be happy about yourself? Ask yourself, "If these are my problem areas, what do I need to do to allow my best qualities to shine forth?" Happiness comes with the proper ATTITUDE. What is the proper attitude?

If you mope around wishing the impossible and wearing baggy, drab clothing, you will look unattractive. You will look larger than you are. You will feel bad. People will ask you if you are all right. There is no end to brooding and complaining. "The grass is always greener on the other side of the fence, but you never know about the thorns until you get there." Someone will always be thinner. Someone will always be more attractive. If you took the time to evaluate yourself, you would find that there is not too much terribly wrong with you. Through a combination of all your finer accents, your more negative ones are outweighed. Be happy with the way you are. That individuality is what makes you unique. However, do not lie to yourself about figure flaws. Know your body. Learn how to disguise flaws or create illusions that detract. By relaxing and feeling content with your new-found knowledge, your mind can work on camouflaging those areas in which you are unhappy. You must respect yourself enough to care about how others see you and how you see yourself. It is all about ATTITUDE.

Do not be afraid to look at yourself. Gaze into the mirror for five to ten minutes. Locate your problem areas. Find your finer features and capitalize on them. So what if you have large hips; your waist looks smaller. If you did not have hips, you would not be a woman. If your arms are too long, focus on the lovely shoulder line or your graceful height. In addition, you do not have to pay to have things shortened. If you have to wear glasses, do not despair. There are some fantastic styles and colors in frames today. Why not make different glasses your trademark? Associates will look forward to seeing your eyes everyday. If your face is round, you have an abundance of wonderful long earrings at your disposal. It will be a joy for others to see what fun earrings you have on each day. If you are large, venture into odd colorations and prints. Bright colors and bold prints will detract from your size and add to your persona. Once you have completed your attitude adjustment, you are ready to learn about smart shopping.

What is a "Smart Shopper"? A smart shopper is the person that knows herself and her closet. She knows what kind of garments are necessary for her lifestyle.

A CLOSET CASE: Birth Of A Wardrobe

Everything in her closet may not have been bought to go together, but she is knowledgeable in how to create coordinating ensembles with what she owns. She is open to change. She never allows herself to be categorized. She buys quality.

To be a really smart shopper, you must first shop your own closet. You must be aware of what you own to have some inkling of what you need to buy (or not buy). We suggest going through each item in your closet and putting it through the "Love it or Leave it" test. The next few pages contain a method of determining if an item is necessary or just taking up space. You will also be able to judge yourself, your previous shopping habits, and your future shopping needs. You will understand why certain items were purchased and why they were good/bad choices for your closet. You will also see what factors motivate your purchases and will be able to screen future purchases through the use of that knowledge. A comprehensive overview of your likes, dislikes, and personality selections will be a portion of your dividends. For the execution of the "Love it or Leave it" test, you will need a pen, a medium sized notebook, a cardboard box, and a camera. Before engaging in the following test, you will require a clear head, quietness for concentration, one free day for yourself, and a strong shot of honesty. When you are prepared with the above, you are ready to proceed. (Note: Answers to all questions should be recorded in your notebook.)

"Love it or Leave it"
Part One

1. What are my best features? ---
   List all areas you wish to accent, consider your best points, or those about which you receive compliments. This list will allow you to know what areas to focus upon when shopping. Your silhouette selection should try to complement these areas.
2. What are my worst features? ---
   List all of the areas you are conscious of, that give you problems while

shopping, that make you feel the worst about yourself. This list allows you to be fully aware of all problem areas. Now you know what areas to focus upon when trying to create illusions. Your silhouette selection should always detract from these areas. Also, use this list when reviewing the next chapter for helpful hints in camouflaging.

3. What colors do I like/dislike? ---

In one column, list the colors you feel you wear well. In the other column, list the colors you dislike. Every woman is aware of her flattering and unflattering colors. Don't let **anyone** talk you into or out of a color. Every person will have a different opinion. You do not need anyone to tell you; just look in the mirror and see how you feel. Every woman can wear every color. You just need to determine the degree of intensity that is most flattering.

4. What colors do I like but feel I cannot wear? ---

Once again, every woman can wear every color. You need to decide what shade(s) within that color's spectrum you can wear. Do not be afraid to try. There are complementary methods to wear colors you find unflattering. Refer to some of the methods noted in the previous chapter.

Part Two

Pull out all of the clothes from your closet and get ready to go through each piece asking the questions listed. Be prepared to try on all of your garments to yield accurate responses.

1. Why did you buy this article of clothing? ---
   (A) Was it the fabrication?
   - Did you choose this garment because of its fiber content?
   - Did the fabric just feel good?
   - Was it something new and different in terms of fabrication?
   - Was it washable?
   (B) Was it the style?
   - Is this a style you are comfortable with and have tried before?

A CLOSET CASE: Birth Of A Wardrobe

- Is it new and exciting in fashion and you just had to have one?
- Is the silhouette flattering for your figure type?
- Does the garment accent/detract from your problem areas?

(C) Was it the color?
- Is this one of your better colors?
- Is it a "hot" new fashion color and your closet had to have it?
- Is it a color that will fit well into your wardrobe?

(D) Was it a good weight?
- Is this suitable for your climate?
- Is this a good fabrication for textural mixing?
- Is the weight comfortable to wear?

(E) Was this purchase on a whim?
- Do you get good wear out of this garment?
- Does it mix with at least five other items in your wardrobe?
- Do you regret this purchase?
- Do most "on a whim" purchases seem like bad choices in hindsight?

2. Select the closet items you don't wear and determine the reason. ---
    (A) Is it too small/large?
    (B) Do you not feel good in it?
    (C) Did you get a bad comment regarding it?
    (D) Is it flattering/unflattering?
    (E) Are you tired of it?
    (F) Maybe it was just a bad purchase.

3. Select the closet items that you wear, but you are not excited about. Why? ---
    (A) Is it too conservative/far out?
    (B) Is it the color?
    (C) Is it the silhouette?
    (D) Is it just old?

4. What items do you love and why? Decide what made you purchase the item. ---
   (A) Was it the color, style, or fit?
   (B) Was it a combination of the three?
5. While wearing, on which outfits have you received compliments?
   (A) Did the look evoke compliments from men and women?
   (B) Did they compliment the color?
   (C) Did they compliment the silhouette?
   (D) Is this a garment you feel good in?
6. Are there any items in your closet that you really like but never wear? ---
   (A) Do you not know how to coordinate them with other items in the wardrobe?
   (B) Have the occasions for that type of outfit not arisen?
   (C) Is it tiring to put the garment on?
   (D) Do you feel that one day you will be able to fit into it, although it is three sizes too small?

Upon reviewing each item in your closet with this questionnaire, you should have a good idea of what type of shopper you are. You also know what shape your closet is in. Furthermore, you know the warning signs of a bad purchase. Now, all of the items you do not wear, do not like, or cannot wear need to be put in that cardboard box. You may sell them, give them away, or stick them in the attic. They are not doing you any good in your closet.

Secondly, photograph all of the items that are left. Divide your book into categories: winter clothing, spring clothing, eveningwear, year-round attire, accessories, shoes, etc. File the photographs into your wardrobe notebook. Usually, people forget everything they own the minute they close the closet door. It is also difficult to remember colors if they are not in front of you. This notebook will assist you when you are shopping. You no longer have to try to remember what is in your closet. You can have it with you at all times. Also, a salesperson can assist you when purchasing a new garment. She can

A CLOSET CASE: Birth Of A Wardrobe

show you how to coordinate the new item with garments you own. Try to group the pictures in categories, as noted earlier. It will be organized and you will be able to locate items quickly. You may wish to use the "Love it or Leave it" test on other items in your wardrobe such as shoes, belts, scarves, and jewelry. Then, photograph these items. By keeping all of this information with you, you are less likely to make incorrect choices. In the long run, you will be more satisfied. This is the best way to yield a wardrobe instead of a closet full of clothing.

Once you have completed setting up your notebook, flip to a few pages before the end. Here is where you place future plans for yourself. Use the following examples as a guide. State the plans that relate to your wardrobe and personality.

- List the basics that your closet needs.
- If your closet holds too many casual garments, change directions. Start buying dressier ensembles.
- If you wish to change your image, set up a folder containing pictures of the type of image you want to portray. Take this folder with you when you shop. It will be of assistance to the salesperson.
- If you are a person that primarily wears earth tones and you want to start wearing brights, list the bright shades that you will feel comfortable wearing. Make yourself purchase a few of these.
- List the colors you have never tried. Make a point to at least go in a store and try them on. You do not have to buy them unless you like the way you look.
- Use the same principle for new styles. If you have never tried a long/short skirt, how do you know what it will look like?

These are just a few examples. You must tailor the questions to meet your own needs. These statements will help you shop. They will provide you the courage to at least try things on. It is amazing what writing something down will do. It is the written word; it is no longer an idea floating around.

There are some shoppers that buy constantly. They have the money, the occasions, and the desire. They may never wear a garment twice. That is fine if it is their lifestyle. However, the majority of housewives and other working women want to build a stable wardrobe and get wear out of their purchases. The notebook you have just completed is a statement of who you are. It is the birthplace of a feminine image that will evolve into a confident fashion-conscious wardrobing expert, an expert that holds the key to unlocking any persona hanging behind the closet doors. She holds a key labeled "Sense of Independence."

"Sense of Independence" pertains to the ability to try new things. Do not let others dictate your fashion. If they are not fashion-forward enough to try a new style, do not let their fear harness your sense of independence. Some of us have to be followers, and some of us have to be leaders. Be a "Leader." You set the standards. You are the future of fashion.

6 BODY SCULPTURE:
Time, Illusion, and Image Formation

— Can I wear asymmetrical styles with my height and weight?

— How can I detract from these hips, when I just want to wear a dress?

— My chest is too small, what can I do?

— I am a very simple person. What kind of style, without too much "frou-frou," will make my shoulders look wider?

— Are there any ways I can maneuver my accessories to assist in creating illusions?

The human eye loves beauty of line. It is proven in the expression of sculpture, painting, architecture, and fashion design. Through the use of various mediums, these art forms are based on the manipulation of line, shadow, and light. Because of the graceful elegance of the human form aligned with its surroundings, Michelangelo's "David" captures a hypnotic gaze from any passerby. Shadow and light epitomize the emotions encased in Leonardo da Vinci's "The Last Supper." The futuristic design of Paco Rabanne, the simplicity and sophistication of Donna Karan, and the intricacy of an Ungaro masterpiece are expressions of each designer's sense of line and proportion. When trying to create an illusion, artists generate products that are appealing to the eye. When a painter wants to make an item look smaller or recessed, he/she will use shadow or a dark color. To create an image of increased size or nearness, an artist will use light colors and/or contouring lines. We can adopt the same principles to stylize illusions in our own lives. Through the use of clothing, we must focus on creating a body line...a body line that the eye is allowed to follow...a body line that creates an illusion. The body line can be expressed through the use of color, fabrication, forced direction, or style lines (design).

Color is a very effective tool in the execution of illusion formation. Through color, you can minimize waist or hip lines, appear taller or shorter, and broaden or decrease the bustline. You may achieve any figure ambition. Your main consideration is to understand how to use color effectively to produce your desired results. There are three primary methods of achieving body lines through color: **singular colorations, multiple colorations** and **color blocking.**

Singular colorations encompass methods, through the use of one dominant color, of creating illusions of increased height and thinness. Of course, this method works best when a silhouette of length is displayed: a long jacket, pants, or a long skirt. If you have on a bolero, bustier, and mini you will not achieve the desired effect. (See Figure 6-1) The first model is wearing a cropped jacket, tank, and a mini skirt. She seems shorter and wider because of the proportion of the pieces in relation to her overall appearance. The eye focuses, mainly,

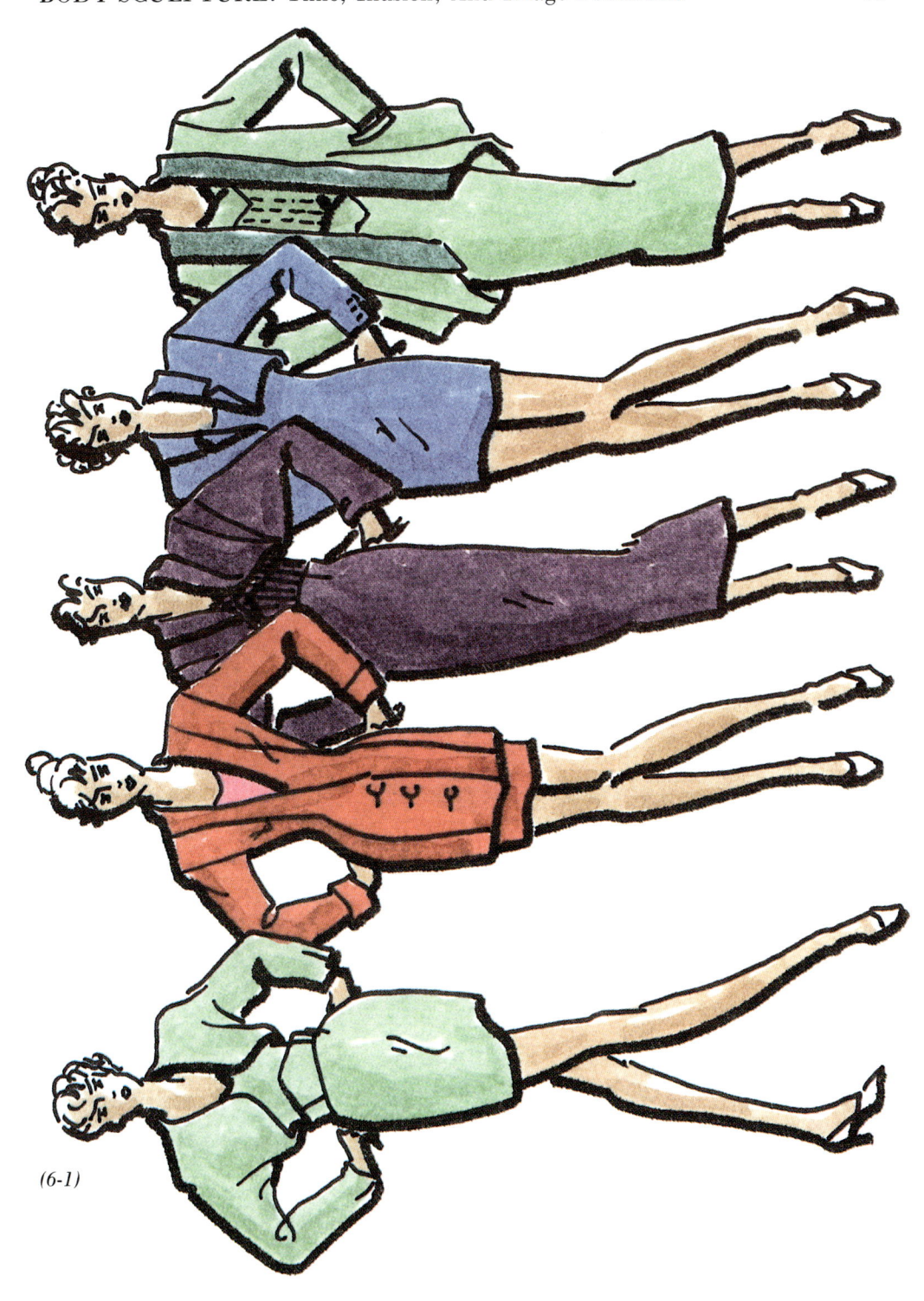

BODY SCULPTURE: Time, Illusion, And Image Formation

(6-1)

on the color-saturated area. Because of the limited length of the garment, the width is prominently presented. The second model is also attired in a tank and mini skirt. However, her jacket is long. What does this do? The longer jacket suggests a feeling of length. The eye is given a line to follow. Because of an illusion, the onlooker attributes a longer waist to the image. The longer jacket makes it more difficult to know exactly where the waist is. The eye establishes a "waist" point, using the length as a guide. Does this mean you should never wear cropped jackets? No. Model 3 has a cropped jacket, bustier, and long skirt. The long skirt makes it difficult to decipher where the knees actually are. The eye establishes a logical "knee" point. This "point" happens to be lower than the actual area. Therefore, your legs look longer, resulting in a taller appearance. Model 3's knees look lower than Model 1's. The fourth model is wearing a tank dress beneath a bolero. Why is this look flattering and Model 1's look unflattering? They seem to be the same. Remarkably, they are not the same. Model 1's ensemble designates a definite waistline. The waistline is another break in an image of broken pieces. Model 4's ensemble does not contain a breaking point at the waist. The tank dress is a continuous piece. Continuity is the strength in an ensemble of this nature. In addition, the cropped jacket allots a higher waist to the image. Thus, the legs look longer. Finally, a long jacket and skirt will create a look of length. In this scenario, the waist appears to be lengthened, the knees appear to be lowered, and an overall taller appearance is attributed to this model's characteristics. Because of the follow through of color on the previous models, the width is narrowed. The longer something is, the narrower it appears. The shorter something is, the greater the tendency to locate width edges for balance. What about pants? The same rules apply. (Fig. 6-2)

The "hotpants" on Model 1 are very short. The lowered neckline of the tank also decreases the longitudinal factor. Although the legs look long, the torso seems "squatty." To create a longer look, we topped this outfit with a fingertip coat. Now, the torso appears longer. Additionally, the legs still look long.

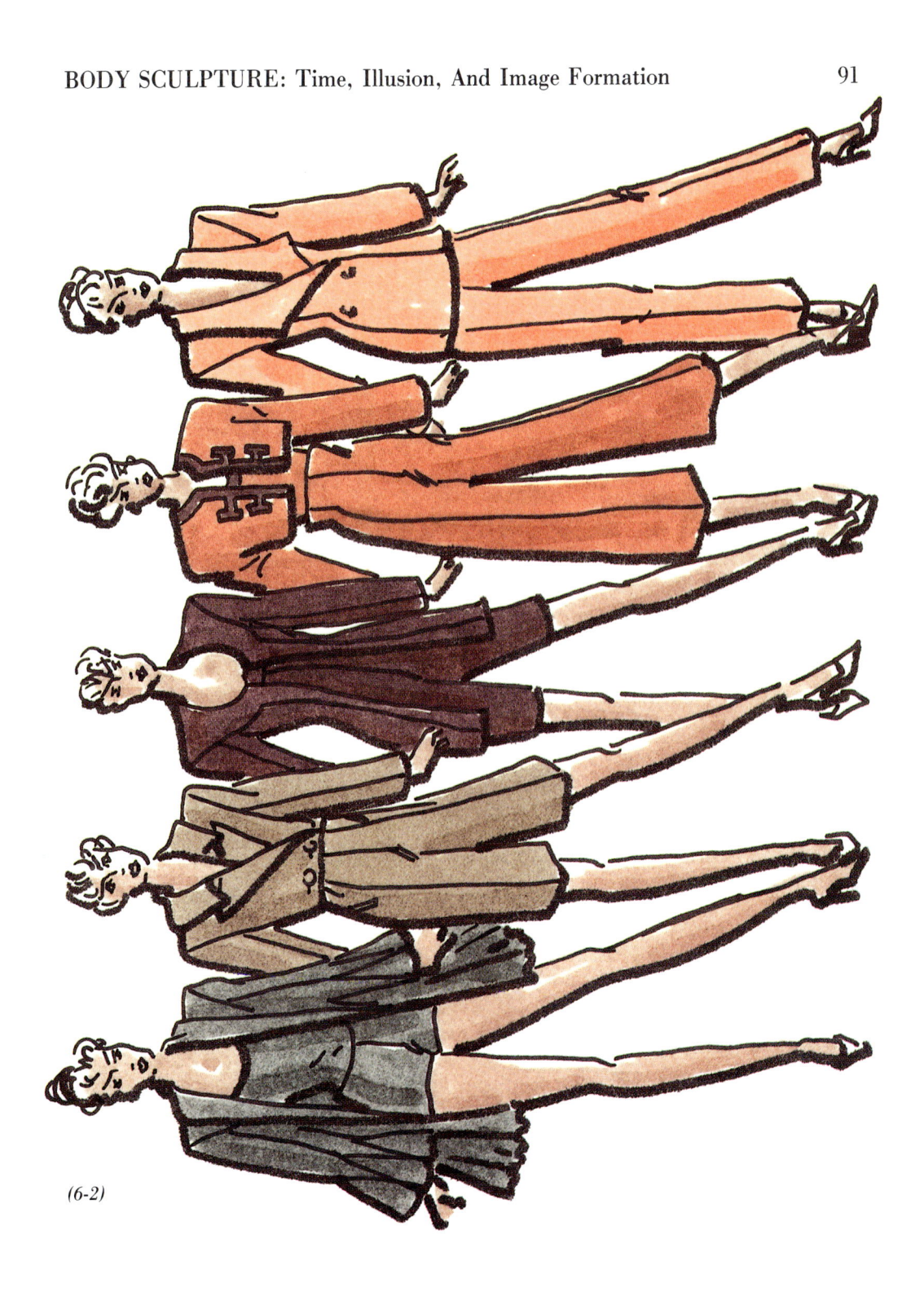

BODY SCULPTURE: Time, Illusion, And Image Formation 91

(6-2)

Model 2 carries the length in the city short. The length from waist to knee is accented by the short coat and exaggerated collar. Let us look at Model 3. Because no waist seams are present in the biker leg unitard, an automatic image of torso length is projected. The jacket reinforces the statement of length. Furthermore, the princess panels of the jacket re-emphasize the leanness of the leg from thigh to ankle. The high waist and tea-length hem are longitudinal factors for Model 4. The knee appears lower and the waist appears higher. The cropped jacket accents these points of sight. The final model is a definition in length, width, and proportion. The same principles apply here as to the fifth skirt model. Also, the substantial collar and use of princess panels assist in the streamlining process. Prints are treated in the same manner. With the correct follow through, increased height and thinness are your rewards. (Fig. 6-3)

Multiple coloration is the second category. Many petite women have declared they are unable to wear multiple color outfits. The reason...multiple colors cut them. Larger size women state multiple colorations make them larger. We have news for all women. These are fallacies. There are many myths and legends regarding fashion. Times are different and you must test every situation before reaching a judgement. By following the principles discussed in the section devoted to singular coloration, multiple colorations can be successfully maneuvered. If you wish to increase your dividends through the use of this concept, color repetition is the road to travel. To create length when wearing multiple colors, you must repeat the color of your blouse below the waistline. An example is to wear a belt of the same color(s) as your blouse. What does this do? Repeating the coloration lowers your waistline and narrows your hipline. Take a look at the models in Figure 6-4. The first model is wearing a multiple

BODY SCULPTURE: Time, Illusion, And Image Formation

(6-3)

coloration involving three colors. There is no belt present, and the waist is well defined. The second model is attired in the same three colors. In addition, she has repeated the color of her blouse in a belt. In comparison, the second model's waist appears longer; thus, creating a taller appearance. The style of belt also played a role. The contoured belt narrowed at the side and dropped in the center. This type of accessory is flattering to every figure. Accessories will be discussed in detail in the forced direction section of the chapter.

(6-4)

BODY SCULPTURE: Time, Illusion, And Image Formation 95

(6-5)

    The next two models illustrate how prints can be integrated into this concept. On the first model, the solid blouse color is echoed in a belt. The second model selects a color from the blouse to use as a belt. When dealing with print, select the base color of the print as the dominant color. Model 3 uses a multicolor belt with the print ensemble. You are not limited in your declaration of a fashion statement. (Fig. 6-5)

Color blocking is the final category in the portrayal of line through color. Color blocking is a method where certain areas of a design are blocked out and replaced with a different, usually contrasting, color. It is a trend that has been prevalent for quite a few seasons. Look at the next three models for a visual description of this definition. (Fig. 6-6) This concept can be derived through the use of any mixture of color. The concept seems very geometric in origin. Geometry is the basis for many designer executions concerning color blocking.

(6-6)

BODY SCULPTURE: Time, Illusion, And Image Formation 97

(6-7)

Aside from the generic form of color blocking, there are stylized color blockings that can assist in illusion formation. Models 1, 2, and 3 illustrate this point rather clearly. (Fig. 6-7) When looking at Model 1, doesn't your eye travel to the seam lines? These seam lines appear to be at her waist edges.

The reason this is carried through successfully is that the brighter color is in the center and the darker color on the outside. She has minimized her waist, hips, and bustline. Her shoulder line has also been narrowed. If she wanted to appear wider, the color concentration would be reversed. Model 2 is an example of this point. The same dress looks completely different and accomplishes different tasks. Now, the shoulder appears wider. There is a defined waist and hip. In addition, the bust seems enlarged. What if you wanted to appear wider in the shoulders but, narrower everywhere else? Model 3 illustrates the method of creating a broader shoulder line. Color allocation and style line are the players on this field. The brighter color is used on the inside. Also, the style line is very wide at the shoulder area. This is the primary reason for the brighter usage of color in the center. Then, the style line steeply narrows toward the bottom of the dress. A darker color is used on the outer limits of the style line. The style line and color provoke your eye to stay focused at the shoulder area, the widest point.

Color blocking travels not only vertically, but also horizontally. (Fig. 6-8) Model 1 wants to increase the bustline. Model 2 wants to decrease hers. To maximize the bustline (Model 1), we carried the darker color just underneath.

BODY SCULPTURE: Time, Illusion, And Image Formation

The eye focus is on the bust and shoulder area. The brighter color brings that section of the body forward. The bust is increased through nonsurgical methods. To minimize the bustline (Model 2), the style line was carried over the bustline and a darker color was used beneath it. The eye focuses on the shoulder area or on the body as a whole. The bust is decreased through nonsurgical methods.

(6-8)

100   EUROFASHION: Unleashing The Designer In You

(6-9)

As mentioned previously, designers have methods of creating wonderfully stylized pieces. Many of the following designs work because they are attuned to an asymmetric theme. Your eye travels directly to the style line. The stylized color blocking also serves purposes of minimizing and maximizing certain areas of the physique. Models 1 and 2 lead your focus to the bustline. (Fig. 6-9) Depending on the allocation of color, results could be increased or decreased bustlines.

BODY SCULPTURE: Time, Illusion, And Image Formation   101

The hips may be a focal point. Model 3's dress minimizes the size of the hipline. Model 4's dress adds to the size of the hipline. As you now know, a different usage of color on these two examples would alter the results. (Fig. 6-10)

(6-10)

Actually, color blocking bleeds through to the next section: body lines through the use of fabrication blending. The same rules apply to using different fabrications of singular or multiple coloration.

Fabric blocking is the method in which portions of a garment are blocked out for replacements of varying fabrications. Although it is more prevalent in singular colorations, it can be accomplished through the use of multiple colors. Fabric blocking could be considered color blocking, just a more subtle form. Look at Figure 6-11 for illustrative definitions. Model 1's outfit is of the same color but has variations of knit weaves existing within the outfit. In combination with style line, the two textures express their own intensities of shadow and light. Depending on the bulkiness of the fabric, the garment can increase or decrease the dimensions of any area, just as color blocking. Model 2 is wearing a combination of knit and woven: silk/cotton knit and silk tussah. In this situation, the knit is used to camouflage a large bustline. This particular silk/cotton knit is of a very fine texture and weight. The tussah has body which is necessary to balance the weight of the bustline. Model 3 is wearing a collection of fabrications: knit weaves, woven jacquards, silk, and gabardine. As you can see, pattern mixes also work well in fabric blocking.

Another method of establishing body lines through fabric is through blending fabrics of varying weights. For example, a broad-hipped person with narrow shoulders would do well to wear a soft skirt and a sweater top. The soft skirt would fall smoothly at the hipline and the sweater top would act as a balancer. To the other extreme, a narrow-hipped, top heavy person should wear "beefier" fabrics on bottom and softer fabrics on top. Working with figure problems will be discussed in more detail later in the chapter. This leads us to the next section in establishing body lines: forced direction.

Forced direction is taking action to create an eye appealing vision. Through imagery, the viewer's eye can be drawn to certain segments of the physique. This concept is not for changing you but enhancing what you have. This is achieved through the use of accessories and the blending of silhouettes.

BODY SCULPTURE: Time, Illusion, And Image Formation 103

(6-11)

Under the category of accessories fall jewelry, belts, hosiery, scarves, and shoulder pads. Simply by layering an accessory piece on the area, you are trying to accent or detract; you are undertaking a type of forced direction.

Jewelry is very easy to handle and little effort is required. Strands of pearls, gold chains, silver chains, beads, and crystals are available in a variety of lengths and sizes. A long chain easily creates a line of length. A thicker chain will add decoration to an otherwise simplistic look. Large millimeter pearls allow for bulk without the weighted down appearance. A collage of strands adds a textural effect. So many illusions can be piloted.

If you are petite, but insist on wearing high necklines, you should use a chain of length to assist on adding height. If you are large-boned, use large size pearls or heavy chains as a counterbalance. Usage of many strands as one can project a slenderized appearance by acting as a point of focus.

Earrings can also work in creating forced direction. A longer earring can offset a round face or short neck. The neck will appear longer and the face slimmer. A long earring will make the neck appear longer if it halts one inch above the shoulder. A round or square "bob" will help fill out a face that is too thin.

Bracelets are wonderful accenting tools. A wide bracelet can act as a cuff, thus shortening an arm that is too long or filling the space of a sleeve that is too short. Many thin bangles will add to the breadth of an otherwise short arm.

Scarves can be manipulated to display any illusion and they look great too. A tied scarf may work as a necklace. When tied in this manner, length is acquired. If the scarf is looped snugly around a thin neck, instant weight is gained. Depending on the coloration, a sash tied at the hip may narrow the width. Through proper execution of concepts discussed in Chapters 4 and 6, a scarf can be considered a wardrobe. (See final page for ordering information on *Accessori Artistri:* a guide encompassing ways to tie and use scarves and other accessories.)

Belts may also be used...Any person can wear a belt. Any size can wear a belt. Every person should not wear every kind of belt. It is important for you to know which type(s) are best for you. We have yet to meet a person that cannot wear a contoured belt. A contoured belt is smaller at the sides than it is in the center front. (Fig. 6-12) The center front is either curved or pointed.

BODY SCULPTURE: Time, Illusion, And Image Formation

(6-12)

The curved is the more wearable of the two. The back of the belt can be the same as the sides or slightly narrower. The most flattering contour belts are one-and-a-half to two inches in width (at the sides). Can you wear a belt that wide? Yes. If the belt were two inches all the way around, we might say no. However, this belt is different widths all of the way around. The center front portion covers the stomach bulge that we all say we have. Secondly, it creates a downward sloping line. This line makes our waists appear smaller, our length

(6-13)

from neck to waist appears longer, and it gives us definition where there is none. In essence, we look taller, slimmer, and shaped. This is also a belt that any age can wear.

There are some variations to the contour belt: drop belts, sculptured belts, and yoke treatments. Drop belts are worn to hang below the waist or contain a section that drops below the waist. (Fig 6-13) The focal point of any belt should always be placed on a princess line of the body. If a drop belt is a waist

BODY SCULPTURE: Time, Illusion, And Image Formation 107

belt, the dangling portion should be placed on the princess line. (See Figure 6-21 for an illustrative definition of the princess line of the body.)

Sculptured belts are those layered, braided, or artsy belts. (Fig. 6-14) These belts usually have a lot of beads, leather, cording, and/or metal hardware on them. They are most flattering if something is hanging from them. They are also complementary if the design carries around the sides of the belt. There should be no center point of focus.

(6-14)

108   EUROFASHION: Unleashing The Designer In You

(6-15)

Finally, yoke treatments are a type of built-in belt. This kind is actually a style line within a garment. (Fig. 6-15) However, it embodies the complementary attributes of a contour belt. The more common term for a yoke treatment at the waist or hipline is "midriff." A midriff can extend above the waist, as well as below. It is most flattering when it is shaped into some type of point, rounded or pointed.

BODY SCULPTURE: Time, Illusion, And Image Formation 109

There is one lesson that is invaluable. You must never wear a belt that focuses the eye in the center of the body. It is the most unflattering item you could ever put on, unless you are in the 2% category of the "absolutely gorgeous" and have the body to match. What do I mean by a belt that focuses on the center? This primarily refers to "buckle" belts. "Buckle" belts are the fabric, leather, skin, and suede belts that have a buckle closure or ornament at the center front waist area. This idea does not refer to any belt containing decoration that carries around the waist, from princess line to princess line. The other type of belt that falls into the nonwearable category are those sculptured belts containing an ornament at the stomach. This type of belt has nothing stemming from the ornamental piece. Why should you not wear these types of belts? When you place something right at the stomach, you draw the eye directly to that portion of your body. The abdomen is the most common area of complaint. If you already have a stomach, a central buckle will just add weight to it. Even if you do not have a stomach, it is likely you will create one with a belt of that styling. This is the only style belt we have found unflattering to most people. Belts are made to accent your figure. They are not meant to be hindrances. It has been proven that the wearing of a belt is a better figure enhancer than not wearing one. If you own belts, pull them out and wear them. If you do not own a belt, go out and buy one. (Fig. 6-16 illustrates the "no-no" in belt science.)

Colored hosiery is a wonderful asset to the fashion industry. There is textured, plain, with feet, without feet, printed, solid, etc. There is no end. There is only fashion-able advancement. If you want to create length, follow through on your color allotment. Substantial color allocation should be concentrated from either hose to shoe or dress to hose. Dress to shoe colorations tend to emphasize your height. If you are tall, you will see nothing but long legs. If you are short, the length from dress to shoes will seem reduced.

With the emphasis on colored hosiery, city short and mini skirt sales have flourished. Longer skirts and pants take on an added sophistication. The use of different types of hosiery is a personal statement of fashion. If you are not used to wearing colored or textured hosiery, you will have to make yourself engage in the activity. It is difficult to start. However, once you start, you cannot stop. By rereading Chapters 4 and 6, you can develop a complete look of "Eurofashion" from head to toe: tonal, contrast, print mixture, or print collaboration.

(6-16)

BODY SCULPTURE: Time, Illusion, And Image Formation 111

(6-17)

The mystery of shoulder pads...There are times when shoulder pads are considered in and times when they are considered out. The fact is, you need to do what is most flattering for you. Do not worry about being out of style. In my opinion, the majority of women could not survive "fashionably" without shoulder pads. (Fig. 6-17)

You can buy all shapes and sizes of shoulder pads: rounded, oval, squared, thick, or thin. First, decide how large a shoulder pad you require. It is best to stay as natural looking as possible. Upon selecting the right size pad for your figure type, you can watch the fashion forecasts to see what shape is "in." For example, the eighties called for a man-tailored, squared-off shoulder pad. The nineties are suggesting a more feminine, rounded, natural look. Whatever the shoulder pad, you will reap the benefit of accentuating lines. A slimmer waist and hip in conjunction with added height are automatic rewards. If you have large hips or a tummy, it is imperative that you use shoulder pads to enhance your appearance. In addition, there are many garments that are long waisted or lacking of pads. It is up to you to add the necessary touches to make yourself and the ensemble look dynamic. Shoulder pads are an investment in dressing. No wardrobe should be lacking them.

Style line interpretation is the final category in the expression of body lines. We are at the mercy of designers, to a certain extent. Since we have to adjust to forthcoming trends and adapt our personalities to burgeoning fashions, we should know our bodies and the silhouettes we can carry. Why not work with silhouettes to achieve our best looks? Then, through blending of silhouettes within the closet, we can shape our personalities to project a certain image.

Look through your closet and try to invent new silhouettes for yourself. Try your long jacket with short and long skirts. Try your long jacket with straight and full skirts. Layer your jackets. Layer a vest under a jacket that is shorter. Put a vest on top of your jacket. Wear a pair of leggings under a front-button skirt. Wear two pair of leggings at the same time. Your closet is at your disposal.

BODY SCULPTURE: Time, Illusion, And Image Formation 113

(Fig. 6-18) To reach this stage of silhouette blending, you must establish what style lines are best for your closet. Skirts and pants are fine examples of style line interpretations for particular figures. Look at the two examples for a better understanding in defining your proper silhouette.

(6-18)

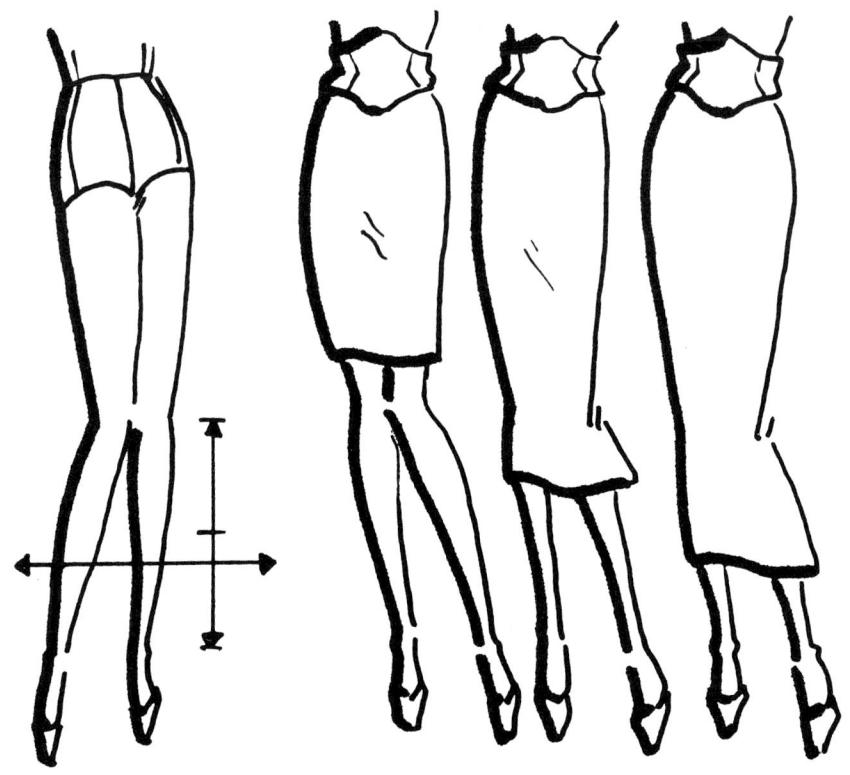

(6-19)

    Probably, the most important factor in purchasing a skirt is establishing a viable length for your height. A longer skirt can be very figure flattering if it does not exceed a certain point. There is no set skirt length at this time. Consequently, anyone can wear any length. If you choose to stick with longer length skirts, you must learn what length not to exceed for your height. There is a certain point on every woman's leg that she should not surpass. It happens to be the same point on every person's leg but, it creates different lengths on different women. (Fig. 6-19) Look at the area, from the middle of your knee to the top edge of your ankle. Find the midway point and add approximately two inches. This measurement may vary, depending on your height. If you are petite, 5'4" and under, you may only add one inch. If you are taller than

5'7", you may add three inches. If a taller woman exceeds this point, she will appear taller. If a petite woman exceeds this point, she will start looking shorter. If it is in your personality to venture beyond these dimensions, feel free to express yourself. Very few people can carry such freedom off successfully.

If you have to wear a full length skirt, what should you do? Taller women's hemlines should cease one inch above the floor. Petite women should use an ankle length hemline. If you are of average height, use the guidelines in adopting a length.

If you are petite and want to wear a short skirt, wear colored hosiery to assist in adding a couple of inches to your height. This is also a good idea for women of average stature. If you are tall and do not wish to look taller, use a contrasting hose color.

Pants encompass another diversified area of fashionable bottoms. Through the reentry of the palazzo pant on the fashion scene, we had many petite women complain that they could not wear them. Contrary to their belief, we found that shorter women looked better in the "cropped" palazzo. In this case, the pant may hit the ankle and still be flattering.

Such a pant actually gives them more height. However, very tall women seemed to have pants on that were too short. Taller women look better in the full length palazzo. If you are of average height, you have the advantage of both styles at your disposal. (Fig. 6-20)

(6-20)

    Then, there is the tapered pant. Most people think a tapered pant makes you look taller and slimmer. It is not always the case. A tapered pant immediately draws attention to your legs. If you are short, they will see it. If you have a stomach, it will be very evident. If you are tall, you will seem like all legs. We are not saying the pant should be flared. We are saying straight legs and sometimes fuller legs are the silhouettes to choose, when trying to create illusions. A full leg will balance out a stomach's size, resulting in an overall focus. The eye will not be focused directly on the problem area. You can always be in style; you just need to find your niche within each silhouette.

BODY SCULPTURE: Time, Illusion, And Image Formation 117

Before entering into the logistics of style line enhancements for figure flaws, there is one style line that is flattering to every figure: large, small, short, or tall. It is the asymmetrical line. Although it is a very flattering line, most people do not use it to its fullest capabilities. Most people are not even aware of its existence. Most garments that are made today are based on the principles of asymmetry and beauty of line.

(6-21)

118 **EUROFASHION: Unleashing The Designer In You**

All asymmetric lines are guided by the princess panels of the body. The princess line is the line equidistant from your side and center front. (Fig. 6-21) Princess lines are the enforcers of body asymmetry, from the subtle to the explicit. You encounter asymmetrical lines in most garments you try on. Once you are aware of these lines, shopping for enhancing silhouettes becomes easier.

(6-22)

BODY SCULPTURE: Time, Illusion, And Image Formation   119

(6-23)

Subtle asymmetry is evident in necklines, jacket closures, and sleeve styling. The greater the degree of angle for a line, the more explicit the asymmetry becomes. Look at Figures 6-22 and 6-23 for insight into the world of fashion, according to asymmetry. These are the lines you should lean toward when choosing a garment.

NOTES

7 "FIGURE"-ATIVELY SPEAKING:
Knowing Your Body

— What styles would be flattering for my large hips?

— Nothing ever fits my long arms.

— How do you decide what styles are appropriate for various figure types?

— Everything I try accents my tummy.

Listed in the following pages are helpful hints in concealing figure flaws. We have tried to concentrate on the most common areas of complaint. Try to follow the hints when you are shopping. You will feel better about yourself and you will see a noticeable improvement in your appearance. Every figure is different and you must use your own judgement to achieve the best possible look.

1. Very Thin Neck --- If your neck is thin, you are an excellent candidate for scarves, chokers, and turtlenecks. Choose bottoms that have extra details and/or trims. Collars will also add weight. (Fig. 7-1)

(7-1)

2. Very Long Neck --- You will do very well with items that fill the neckline. You can wear scarves, jewelry, and clothing with breadth. You will also wear larger earrings very well. Different types of collars are at your disposal. On the other hand, you may wish to bring out the beauty of a long neck rather than concealing it. Sometimes the opposite solution is the most eye appealing. Wear interesting necklines: sweetheart, portrait, puzzle. There are tribes existing in Africa whose goals are for women to have very long necks. They stretch

"FIGURE"-ATIVELY SPEAKING: Knowing Your Body

the neck to achieve such an appearance. You are lucky enough to already have it. (Fig. 7-2)

(7-2)

3. Very Short Neck --- Styles that will create the illusion of a longer neck are what you need to focus on. You can use chains, V-necks, scoop necks, cardigans, collarless jackets, and jackets with long collars. A short hair style may also be a part of your look. (Fig. 7-3)

(7-3)

4. Sloping/Narrow Shoulders --- You need styles that will create width or assist in drawing the eye elsewhere. Your first investment should be in a variety of shoulder pads. Once you have created a shoulder line, you can concentrate on silhouette design and fabric texture. Bulky and/or textured fabrications will add body to the shoulder area. In most cases, when the eye is drawn to a shorter area, the width is increased. This is the concept you must remember when shopping for silhouettes. Focus on boleros, boxy jackets, short-haired furs, short fringing, small collars, and yokes. You can also make your shoulders appear wider by baring them. However, the style line concentration should stay at the base of the neck. Halter styles will work well for you. Also, camisoles with very thin straps can assist. (Fig. 7-4)

(7-4)

"FIGURE"-ATIVELY SPEAKING: Knowing Your Body   125

5. Broad Shoulders --- You need styles that create length and draw the eye inward. Stylized shoulder lines will be the best way for you to start. Work with color blocking (as discussed in the previous chapter). Work with shoulder lines within your actual shoulder line: raglans, dolmans, and kimonos, for example. Dropped and exaggerated armholes will also create illusions of length. The longer the length of an item, the shorter the width will appear. For this reason, you should try to focus on longer jackets or jackets with long slim collars. V-necks, scoop necks, and asymmetrical looks are also lines of detraction. (Fig. 7-5)

(7-5)

6. Slim Arms --- You do not need anything that outlines your arms. If you wear items that are fuller and larger, you will seem to have fuller arms. Wearing bulky fabrications will add body to you. If you do not want the weight of bulkier fabrics, try full, flowing, billowy sleeves. Color blocked and/or seamed sleeves can also be a solution. Cuff treatments are very good as well. Elbow length or long sleeves will wear your arms best. (Fig. 7-6)

126   EUROFASHION: Unleashing The Designer In You

(7-6)

7. Heavy Arms --- You need to stay away from the armholes that are too small and constricting. Never wear an item that is tight. Full sleeves and style lines are very appropriate: dolmans, raglans, drop shoulder treatments, and gusset sleeves. You will also be flattered by dropped armholes and elongated, open necklines. (Fig. 7-7)

(7-7)

"FIGURE"-ATIVELY SPEAKING: Knowing Your Body

8. Very Long Arms --- Just remember length can be counteracted by width and dissection. Try color blocking through the use of color and/or texture. Chunky jewelry and wide cuffs will also be helpful. Additionally, try variations on fuller sleeves. Stay away from sleeveless, 3/4 length, and clingy silhouettes. (Fig. 7-8)

(7-8)

9. Very Short Arms --- You should stick to solid sleeves that create a continuous line. We are not saying you must stay away from print, texture, or style lines; you just need to carry through whatever you decide to use. Any shorter length would also be a flattering sleeve silhouette: cap sleeves, elbow sleeves, or 3/4 sleeves. Stay away from chunky jewelry and wide cuffs. (Fig. 7-9)

128　　　　　　　　EUROFASHION: Unleashing The Designer In You

(7-9)

10. Top Heavy --- Diagonal lines are probably your best accent tool. You will look excellent in surplus wraps, asymmetrical jackets and style lines, double breasted treatments, and vertical color blocking. Also try wearing elongated necklines, elongated scarf tie variations, and jewelry that expresses length. Layering can also be quite beneficial (jackets, cardigans, and vests - preferably with "V" necks). (Fig. 7-10)

(7-10)

"FIGURE"-ATIVELY SPEAKING: Knowing Your Body

11. Flat Chested --- Layering is the best concept for you, too. Any type of jacket is comfortable, adding, and chic. Blouson styles or garments with extra detailing will also be helpful. Clinched waists and bottom interest garments will detract from the chest. Finally, and most importantly, use shoulder pads with everything. (Fig. 7-11)

(7-11)

12. Short Waisted --- Short waisted women need to create the illusion of a longer waist and a taller person. It is a lot simpler than you may think. Longer jackets are the easiest way to start and they are most flattering. You may also wish to try a longer skirt or cropped palazzo pant with that. The use of a contoured belt will definitely lengthen the waist. Additionally, the repetition of the blouse color below the waist (a belt or bottom silhouette) will add height. Elongated necklines, layering, shifts, and hip-hugger bottoms will also create the illusion of length. (Fig. 7-12)

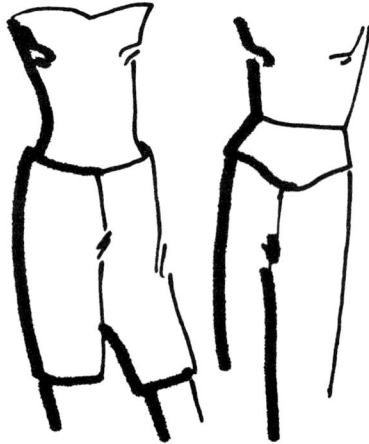

130 EUROFASHION: Unleashing The Designer In You

(7-12)

13. Long Waisted --- You need items that will break the length and still feel comfortable. Actually, long waisted women can wear almost any fashion silhouette. Your length is an advantage. If you feel it is a burden, there are many tricks you may employ. Through the use of color blocking or any break in fabric and/or texture, you will expound on width proportions and minimize length. Layering will help. When purchasing, try to focus on silhouettes with width: short jackets, high-waisted silhouettes, wide belts, and flat to mid heel shoes. Stay away from very thin belts or jewelry. (Fig. 7-13)

(7-13)

"FIGURE"-ATIVELY SPEAKING: Knowing Your Body 131

14. Thick Waist --- This is a very common problem with some very simple solutions. If you are the type of person that likes to cover up, try layering. But, always wear your jacket open. Try blouson silhouettes and chemises/tunics. Your main objective is to create a waist where there is none. The most exciting way to flatter a thick waist is through the use of contoured belts. They make you appear longer waisted, slimmer in form, and illusory of a waist curvature. Asymmetric lines that venture across the waist area are also deceiving of a waistline. (Fig. 7-14)

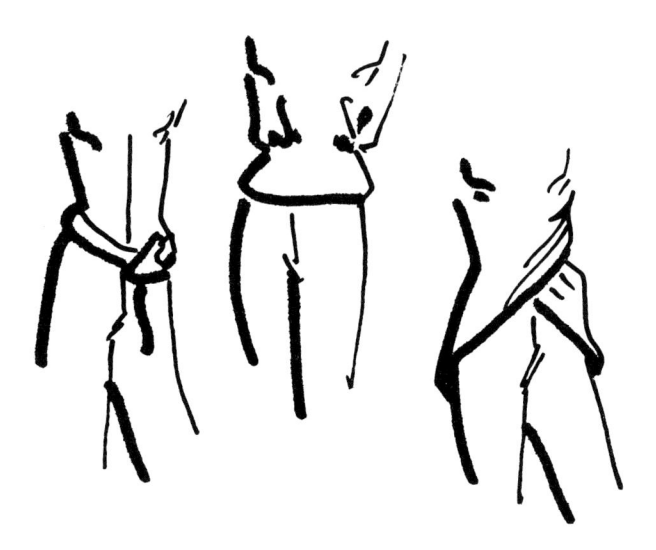

(7-14)

15. The Tummy "Ache" --- Everyone we have ever met complains about a tummy (legitimate or not). Layering is the easiest way to start: jackets, vests, diagonally wrapped scarves, and tunics. A variation of layering is the peplum silhouette. It can do wonders. Peplums conceal the abdominal area. Also, try asymmetrical lines across the abdomen. Here again, contoured belts are an essential for your wardrobe. Pads for the shoulders are a second "must." Basics such as dirndl skirts, stitched down pleated skirts, and softly pleated pants will be comfortable and easy. For a step on the wild side, venture into sarong skirts, jazzy wraps, surplus jackets, and double breasted silhouettes. (Fig. 7-15)

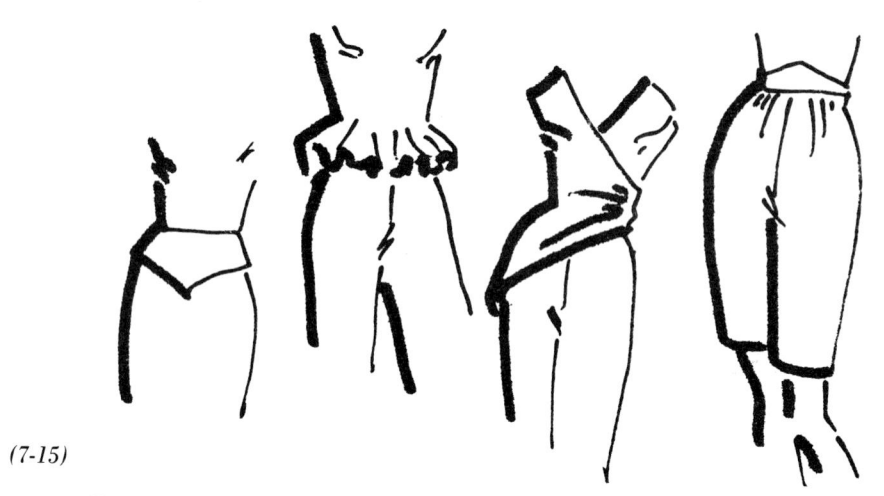

132 EUROFASHION: Unleashing The Designer In You

(7-15)

16. Large Hips --- This section may also be helpful for those women with a large derriere. First, buy some shoulder pads. It would be wise for you to buy blouses and jackets with extra detailing. The detailing will act as a deter-

(7-16)

rent. Any silhouette with length will be helpful: long jackets, long skirts, and cropped palazzo pants. Your best bet would also be to stick with lighter weight fabrications for bottom dressing. Do not buy bottoms with too much detailing such as embroidery, pockets, or side pleats. The exceptions would be contoured yokes, skirts with central panels, and all over pleated skirts. If you have large hips, your waist will look smaller. By focusing attention there, you can have fun with a lot of great belts, as well as, detract from your hips. (Fig. 7-16)

When you find yourself questioning another area of concern, remember how you handled similar situations and use your judgement. Also, remember the principles of length and width. To affect the appearance of length, use varying proportions of width. The more width you use will shorten the optics of length. The more length you use will slim down the optics of width proportions. The proportions of length and width can be directed through the use of clothing, accessories, fabrications, and colorations. With the knowledge of figure-related flaws and the addition of a positive attitude, your sense of independence is free to perform. It is timidity, lack of inspiration, ignorance of change, and fear that hold most people back from their true personalities. You have the knowledge. Do not let anything else hold you back.

NOTES

8 "SIZE"-MIC PROPORTIONS:
Coming To Terms With Numbers

— I am a size "12" (although you can obviously see I am a size "16").
— Surely everyone will know if I buy a larger size.
  I could not possibly do that. Let me see if I can squeeze into the smaller one.
— This suit must be sized wrong. I know what size I wear. How dare you even suggest that I may not be able to fit it!
— Is it true that more expensive garments run larger than cheaper garments?

The most flattering thing you can do for yourself is buy the **right** size. We have found people to be too hung up on numbers. When purchasing footwear, people allow themselves to suffer, just to buy a smaller size. Toes are squeezed into a narrow, because it is a "narrow." When selecting hosiery, some women find themselves on the borderline or just into the next size. Still, they insist on buying the smaller size. Then, complaints arise about the quality of the hosiery. In clothing, women feel depressed to go to the next size. Some women feel depressed to wear their "actual" size. What is a number??? Don't you realize, by wearing tight clothing, you look larger? You should buy what "fits" your body. No one else knows what size you are wearing. The size label is not sticking out of the seam. It is not plastered to your forehead. The salesperson is not going to publish it in your state newspaper. Wear what fits your body.

Do not say "no" to a garment just because the number may be a little larger. Do not embarrass yourself or the salesperson by trying to squeeze into a size twelve if you are undoubtedly a size eighteen. Use the assistance of a salesperson to guide you in selecting garments for your figure. The salesperson is knowledgeable about which brands run larger and which ones are skimpy. Many manufacturers use different measurements for the same size. In one collection, you may wear a twelve. In another collection, you may wear a fourteen. In a third brand, you may fit into an eight. We have one customer that wears sizes four through ten in the same brand. Size depends on the brand, silhouette, fabrication, and labelling. There are many factors that determine how an item will fit your figure.

Fabrications vary in the amount they stretch. Cotton usually runs small. It also has a greater chance of shrinking. Wool crepes have more give. A knit will stretch, but is it showing what you want to show? Silks have no give. If you wear a silk garment that is too tight, it will **shred**. Linens also tend to run small. If you wear a ramie or linen garment that is too small, you will stretch the fabric out of shape. This stretching, in turn, will weaken the fibers. Soon, the garment will be unwearable. You must take care of your garments

"SIZE"-MIC PROPORTIONS: Coming To Terms With Numbers

if you expect them to take care of you. Any garment that is worn, if it is too tight, will weaken. The wearing, in addition to cleaning, will disintegrate the fabric. The garment will have served one third to one half its actual life span.

Something else you may not be aware of is that pattern measurements are inherent to the times. As time has passed, the shape of women has changed. Women's shapes in the 1900's were accentuating of tiny waists, bustle backs, and padded bustlines. As time progressed, bust, waist, and hip measurements changed. The 1960's are reminiscent of "Twiggy-ness." The 1960's meant boyish figures, very slim silhouettes, and flat bustlines. The 1990's signify a well proportioned figure kept up by a healthy outlook. From this form, grading up and down of the measurements establishes proper sloper measurements. These sloper measurements are used in the design and execution of the garments you see in the stores.

Brand also determines the size you will wear. Some designers will select a size eight form and call it a six. This makes you, the customer, feel very good and buy the outfit. Haven't you ever bought a garment because of the size it happened to be? Have you ever repeated this statement, "I should buy this just for size and the fact that I got in it." Some say the higher the price, the smaller the size. Such a philosophy is veritably correct. You will wear a smaller size in a designer garment than in a less expensive piece. All of this is due to the form-size-adjustment. It is also due to the extra ease those houses allot to each garment.

Another determining factor in the sizing of a garment is human error. Human hands sew and tag the sizes onto a garment. It is possible to sew a size four label into a size twelve dress. A size twenty-four label can be placed into a size twenty garment. Recently, a customer came in to match a blouse to an old suit. We matched a turquoise blouse to it. When she put the blouse on, it almost fell off of her. She was a size eight. The tag on the outside of the blouse said size eight. However, the size stamped inside the blouse was a size eighteen.

We are sure the size eighteen woman that bought the blouse felt wonderful fitting into a size eight. Yet, we all know she is an eighteen. She knows too. Just wear what fits.

9 QUALITY LIVING:
To Buy or Not To Buy

— Why do her clothes always look so nice?

— I wonder why this linen suit is one hundred dollars more than the one I bought. It looks the same to me.

— I hate it when my knit pants stretch out of shape and get those little lint balls. What can I do?

— What are some characteristics of a quality garment?

We have learned about color, blending, silhouette enhancement, and the mixing of the three. Next is an introductory course in quality.

There is nothing wrong with a bargain if it is actually a bargain. If someone gives you a basket of peaches and all of them are rotten, it is hardly a bargain. You should not buy something because it is inexpensive. You should not buy something because it is expensive. You should buy quality that will wear well and perform in the way you desire. Get the quality for what you are spending, whether it is ten, one hundred, or one thousand dollars.
Look at the case study below.

> Steph needed to purchase a suit for a job interview. After looking in various places, she narrowed the decision to two suits. Both suits were raw silk and were beautiful shades of emerald green. One suit was a great deal cheaper than the other. However, the cheaper suit was lined and the more expensive one was not. Which one would you have chosen? Steph was perplexed. As a recent graduate, she considered it more economical to go with the less expensive suit. And, after all, it was lined. Steph bought the suit and went to her first interview. By the end of the day, the hip area of the skirt and lower portion of the jacket were extremely wrinkled. The next day, Steph sent the suit to the cleaners. When she got the suit back, it had lost much of its body and looked like an old suit. It was not the dry cleaner's fault. Steph had to go purchase another suit. She went back and bought the other suit. That was five years ago. She is still wearing the second suit. It still looks like new.

Buying a garment does not mean that the purchase is equivalent to every other garment. There is a difference between popular priced, moderate, better, designer, and couturier clothing. The first is in the fabrication. There are many grades of fabric, just as there are many grades of beef. Certain fabrications are woven more intricately. They hold together and retain a particular hand. Cheaper grade fabrications may be woven less intricately. Some fabric is from a better source and is more refined.

The first suit Steph bought was of lower grade silk. It was loosely woven, had pilling tendencies, did not retain dyestuff as well, and was thinner. All of these factors resulted in the fading, pilling, and wrinkling of the garment. The lining was put into the suit to allow it to appear with more body.

Did you know that an unlined suit is more expensive to make than a lined suit? It has to be finished very cleanly inside. The fabric must have enough body to survive on its own. There are companies that specialize in unlined suits. They are so beautifully done; it is a shame you cannot wear them inside out so that everyone can see.

Of course, there are exceptions to the rule. We are not saying that everything expensive is of quality and that everything inexpensive is not. And, we did not say that you should invest only in unlined suits. We are saying use your judgement and purchase a quality garment. In most cases, there is a reason a dress will cost a hundred, a thousand, or ten thousand dollars. It depends on the construction, the fabric, the trimmings, and the reputation of the company. All of these concerns run together to determine the cost of a garment.

What role does construction play? Did you know that it is more expensive to make suit "A" than it is to make suit "B"? (Fig. 9-1)

142   EUROFASHION: Unleashing The Designer In You

(9-1)

QUALITY LIVING: To Buy Or Not To Buy

There is more wastage of fabric when making suit "A." When laying out fabric and preparing for cutting, the cutter must make sure that pattern pieces run on the appropriate grain lines. In order for all pieces to be cut on the same grain, they need to be spread out. In turn, this arrangement leaves a lot of unused fabric space. In addition, there are fewer seams in this garment. It is imperative that the sewing be impeccable. Fewer seams mean there is more attention on these points. As always, there are exceptions to the rule. Patchwork jackets require an excess of sewing. Extra sewing causes the price to go up. Also styles with unusual style lines, jagged edges, and curves contribute to wastage of fabric, complex sewing, and intricate design. The cost goes up again.

What role does fabric play in the cost? As stated previously, fabric comes in a variety of grades. Have you noticed how some knit pants stretch out at the knees, pill, and fade? Then, there are other brands that wear very well. A knit is usually of a better grade when it is of a heavier weight and tighter construction (this refers to interlocks). Some wool gabardines are accused of becoming flat and shiny after cleaning. The better quality of gabardine that you buy, the less chance you will have incurring these problems. By studying the quality of fabric in garments of various price ranges, you will gain understanding of the difference in weight, weave, density, and quality. Price and quality can be affected for the other reasons.

> Susan found a lovely floral skirt to wear with a linen blouse she had purchased. The skirt was priced at one hundred and thirty-five dollars. She happened to come across a replica of the skirt in a less expensive shop. Although the color designation was the same, the colors were a bit lighter. The lighter skirt was thirty dollars. She contemplated which skirt to buy. The blouse cost her one hundred and twenty-five dollars. Why do you think there was such a difference in the price? What would you have done?

The more expensive skirt was of a silk/rayon blend. This skirt's floral pattern had been woven in. For this reason, the skirt had body and draped well on the figure. The less expensive skirt was an acetate that had been printed. The weight of the fabric did not equal in the two skirts. The thirty dollar skirt was a bit lighter. It is a personal decision as to which one you would buy. However, if you had spent that much on the blouse, why would you cheapen it by purchasing a skirt of lesser quality? Furthermore, after a few cleanings, the printed skirt may lose some of its color and much of the body it had initially.

The most important question in a situation like this is one of self-satisfaction. You have to feel good about what you are wearing. Are you going to worry about how you look when you are in a crowd?

Beaded, and knitted fabrications also vary in price and quality. These fabrications can be derived through machine or hand. Of course, a hand knit sweater is likely to cost more than a machine knit. A hand beaded garment is likely to cost more than a machine beaded one. You should look at a garment carefully before deciding the price justifies the quality. There will be some incidents where a machine knit or beaded item may equal or surpass the quality of a hand made item. Bear in mind all quality concerning factors.

Finally, stick to brands with which you are familiar. Shop at establishments that are reputable. If you have been happy with the quality and look of garments from a particular store, stick with that establishment. Patronage will induce a feeling of dedication, a constant effort to keep you happy, and a commitment to quality.

The care of a garment is of the utmost importance in contributing to the life of a garment. Excessive dry cleaning of a garment will make it limp, weak, and tired looking. The best investment you can make is to purchase a steamer. Not only will it save your clothing, it will save your bank account. Clothing does not need to be dry cleaned after every wearing. You can wear certain garments at least two to three times before putting it through the torture of dry cleaning.

Another choice you have is one of washing. Many manufacturers put dry clean labels in their garments to protect themselves. Many garments are hand washable or machine washable (gentle). Educate yourself thoroughly on the fabrication before undertaking the wash. In addition, after your clothing is cleaned, it should be kept in a dark, cool, dry place.

Light affects color in a variety of ways. It can fade or darken a color, depending on the fabrication and dye used. Also, clothing should be kept out of the reach of sunlight when not being worn. Knits and other stretchable materials should be folded and boxed. They can also be placed in tinted sweater bags. It is a waste to spend good money on your clothing if you cannot properly care for it.

Some manufacturers are good scam artists. They try to pass off garments lacking of quality but, encrusted with fantasy. Excessive stoning, jewelling, or fantastic design are no good if the outfit falls apart after the first wearing. Do not buy something because it is "cute." Do not settle for anything less than you deserve. Manufacturers owe you quality, and that is what you should get.

There are particular elements of quality you should keep in mind while shopping. The garment should be finished well. It should be lined. If it is not lined, the inside should look good enough to wear on the outside. Seams should be clean and should not pucker. Reinforced stitching should be present on areas of tension: splits, corners, facings, etc. Does it look like a well made garment? Very few companies leave large inseams anymore. Yet, there are some that still respect the satisfaction derived from purchasing a quality garment. If the garment has wide inseams, it is almost a guarantee of a good garment. Judge the fabric. The weight of the fabric should be heavy enough for the type of silhouette. Look at the trimmings. Have they used a metal or plastic zipper?

Metal zippers are better than plastic ones. Do the buttons equal the rest of the garment?

    The moral of the story is "Buy one, but buy a good one. Then, know how to properly wear and care for your purchase." If you have to spend a little more, go ahead. It may pinch at the time of purchase. In the long run, you will be happier. The most important thing is self-satisfaction. If you feel good about yourself and your clothes are serving you in the manner you desire, you will look beautiful. But, there is one thing we are sure of: if you are standing in a crowded room, you can tell who is wearing quality and who wishes they were.

10 HEALTHY DRESSING:
A Sight For Sore Eyes

— I never go anywhere. Why should I dress up?

— Why can't I wear things like that?

— She always looks so good!

— Did you see how casually she was dressed? She must not be feeling well.

— I still have things hanging in my closet with the tags on.

"I never go anywhere; why should I dress up?" This is a very common statement heard from many people. Why do you need to go anywhere to dress up? You should dress well for yourself. You should treat yourself to pretty things. You should dress well for others. You should allow others the sight of the pretty things you own.

People shop for many reasons, among which are need, desire, occupation, depression, and happiness. The most common reason people shop, quite honestly, is to give themselves a lift. It makes a person feel good to have a new suit or dress. You walk in a different way. You talk in a different way. You act differently. You stand with confidence. You view life with newness. Clothing is directly related to your mood of the day. If you are feeling depressed and put on an old, sloppy bathrobe, you will drag yourself further into the depths of despair. In contrast, if you put on a cheerful ensemble that you feel good in, your whole day will take on a new approach.

A constant routine of good grooming habits and dressing well enables people to remain active and healthy. When you look good, you feel good. When you feel good, you stay active. When you stay active, your body stays healthy. As a healthy person, you can contribute to the well being of other people's lives. There is no end to dressing down. Your goals should be to reach a higher plateau in any undertaking. If you condition yourself to always dress well and stay well groomed, such care will become a natural way of life. You will not want to look any other way. People will also expect you in that way. If you are used to being dressed up and on one occasion you dress very casually, you will educe a rise out of those who know you. Your different dress will be a topic of discussion throughout the day. Some friends will ask if you are feeling well. Some will wonder if you are taking the day off. Many will only stare in awe. People get used to seeing things in a certain light. You must decide what image to take on. There are methods of being dressed up in a casual way.

If you are used to being very casual, jeans and t-shirts, and on one occasion you wear a nice dress, hat, shoes, and jewelry, your friends will be stunned.

HEALTHY DRESSING: A Sight For Sore Eyes

They will think you are going somewhere. You won't be able to dress up for no reason at all. Questions and odd glances will drift your way throughout the day. Isn't that aggravating? Do not categorize yourself. Do not let others have reason to categorize you. Establish a well-dressed image.

Dressing well serves another purpose: it is a symbol of authority. Clothing emits feelings characteristic of the look you are wearing. Many teachers complain they do not have control over their classes. Dressing has a lot to do with it. If you are attired in jeans and a t-shirt or casual pants and tops, you will not fit the image that is embedded in a child's mind. That child will not have respect for your authority. The child will also be less likely to pay attention to anything you have to say. Children can tell you who is dressed nicely. Amazingly, they pay attention to clothing. A teacher does not have to be formally dressed. She should, however, have a skirt and blouse or something to that effect. For those teachers that dress well, authority and attention span are part of the daily curriculum. Male teachers should have dress pants, a shirt, and tie.

For professionals, dressing well can make or break a deal. Your clothing depicts your ability, confidence, and educational stature. A brilliant attorney can come across incorrectly to a judge and jury if she does not project a particular image. Some occupations allow adventure in dressing, whereas, others do not. Whether your job allows conservative or fashion-forward dressing, you should always signify femininity, elegance, intelligence, and ability. Above all remember, you are wearing not only for yourself, but also for those around you.

As we said in the beginning, you should dress for yourself and you should dress for others. Friends and strangers get a lift when they see a well dressed you. Seeing you every day is a pleasure. They look forward to seeing what you will have on next. Your example also raises their aspirations of dressing well. You are a method of staying in touch with fashion without having to go beyond the realm of the immediate. As their awareness grows, curiosity leads them to other sources of inspiration. Dressing well is contagious. Consciousness strengthens a desire to explore new avenues of education in fashion.

There are two sources which, we feel, every woman must treat themselves to: *Women's Wear Daily (WWD)* and *Big Beautiful Woman (BBW)*. *WWD* is considered the "bible" of the fashion industry. It is a daily newspaper that keeps in touch with the latest designers, trends, colors, fabric, and business from the accessory to footwear to apparel markets. Although it is typically considered a trade paper, *WWD* is a virtual gold mine to the uneducated consumer. To unleash the designer in you, you must expose yourself to sources of new design and inspiration. Catalysts are a necessary progression in any learned process.

The second recommended reading is *Big Beautiful Woman, BBW*. *BBW* is intended for "Big" "Beautiful" "Women." However, regardless of size, everyone deserves to read this wonderful magazine. It is an inspirational source for establishing pride in oneself. A great builder in self esteem, *BBW* enables all women to unlock the beauty on the outside after starting from within. *BBW's* statement of policy, alone, is worth the cost of the magazine. The editor's column is an added bonus.

No matter what size, shape, or color, you will benefit from the information in both of these sources. They will serve as guides to self confidence along with their educational attributes. You will also be able to develop a strong sense of independence.

Sense of independence is of key importance in the structuring of a strong fashion image. You should feel comfortable in any garment purchased. Do not let anyone tell you what to wear. After all, you are the one wearing it. If you establish a certain image for yourself and stick by it, others will grow accustomed to it. We have encountered many women that are ruled by their husbands, mothers, bosses, and social circles. There is no happiness for this kind of person. We realize that we must make our husbands (and others) happy, but not at the expense of losing our personalities. Listen to what he has to say. Then, blend likings of both tastes into ensembles until you modify his views. And, you will. Men have the ability to pick up on things just as easily as women.

HEALTHY DRESSING: A Sight For Sore Eyes

As you mold your own fashion image, assist him in stating his fashion consciousness. Try things that are not, necessarily, characteristic of your lifestyle or your liking. If you are a solids person, try some prints once in a while. Slowly integrate new ideas, concepts, and design into your wardrobe. At the same time, leak some of the same types of things into your spouse's wardrobe. There will be a noticeable rejuvenation in your closets and appearances. This newness will filter into your love life, leisure time, and work schedule. Fashion is all about educating, not changing. No one should change you. Your fashion mold should be enhanced. Furthermore, you should share your knowledge.

NOTES

11 SELF-EXPRESSION:
Ruling Out Myths, Legends, and Others' Opinions

— Older women should not wear short skirts should they?

— Isn't it amazing how good men look in color?

— Edna dresses as if she is 150 years old. Someone should tell her.

— Is it true that Mothers-of-the bride can wear prints?

— What is in? What is out?

One problem that many people have is dressing older than they actually are. It is unfortunate that society establishes barriers for particular age groups: dress, career, athletic activities. But things are changing. There are various age groups engaging in strenuous aerobic exercises, rapid river canoeing, sky diving, and stylish dressing. And, why not? As you get older, life is supposed to get better. Every stage of life should be stretched to its fullest potential. Don't dress older than you are.

If you are nineteen, don't dress as if you are thirty. If you are thirty-five, don't dress as if you are fifty. If you are seventy, don't dress as if you are seventy. Dress for the personality you have. Dress for the lifestyle you live. Dress for the future you wish to encounter. If you have great legs at fifty years old, wear skirts above the knee. Show those legs off. Short skirts were made for those people with great legs. If you are ninety-two and love bright colors and large floral prints, put them on. Color is a fountain of youth to be sampled. Bright and bold colors are not characteristic of young people. Bright, bold prints are tributes to the wonders of nature. A ninety-two year old has more right to nature's wonders because of her longer life of experiencing these beauties. If a seventy year old loves long dusters, fur-trimmed suits, and high-heeled ankle boots, why should anyone deny her rights to be stylish, elegant, colorful, and ...alive. Fashion is all about enjoying yourself. Fashion should be fun, no matter what the age. Why fall victim to the fashion "myths"?

Many myths surface with the times. The "yes"s and "no"s of fashion alter with the establishment of new fashion leaders and their media representation. Unfortunately, readers and viewers tend to consider those statements as law. It is up to us to break the bonds of fashion myths. We should create personal interpretations of existing ideas. Become the artist and paint the canvas.

...There was a time when blue and green were considered incompatible.

...There was time when a woman did not leave her abode without hat and gloves.

SELF-EXPRESSION: Ruling Out Myths, Legends, And Other's Opinions

...There was a time when large size women were to be confined to unattractive shrouds of detestable fabrications.

...There was a time when petite women were restricted to petite prints and petite jewelry.

...There was a time when subdued tones and prints were to hide and seal away the aged.

...There was a time when men who wore color and stylish fashions were not considered men.

...There was a time when horizontal stripes were thought to increase the width.

...There was a time when suede was for winter, and linen was for spring.

...There was a time when metallics were strictly for the evening.

...There was a time when white would send people running into the confines of a black garment for slenderization.

...There was a time when Mothers-of-the bride had to wear the same length dress as Mothers-of-the groom.

...There was a time when black and white were considered inappropriate for a wedding.

...There was a time when black was the only justifiable color for a funeral.

...There was a time...

...There was a time...

Someday, today's focus of fashion will also fall into the pit of "There was a time..."

YOU *are* beautiful. YOU hold the knowledge. Make your own creations. Be independent. Remember, YOU are *never* wrong. YOU have the ability to distinguish yourself from others. YOU are a self-sufficient person on the way to becoming the designer of your domain. *YOU are the future of fashion! YOU ARE THE FUTURE OF EUROFASHION... UNLEASH THE DESIGNER IN YOU!!!*

ILLUSTRATION INDEX

1-1	New York skyline influence,	11
1-2	Egyptian pyramid/geometric influence,	12
1-3	Spanish abode influence,	13
1-4	Gourmet meal/source of inspiration,	14
1-5	Gourmet meal inspired sportswear,	15
1-6	Gourmet meal inspired tailoring,	17
1-7	Gourmet meal inspired eveningwear,	18
1-8	Gourmet meal inspired colorations,	19
1-9	Gourmet meal inspired prints,	20-21
2-1	Print swatches of ethnic influence,	26-27
2-2	Environmental influence swatches/abstract,	27
2-3	Environmental influence swatches/defined,	28
2-4	Social conscious awareness influences,	29
3-1	Color chart of A, B, C, & D color families,	36
3-2	Color chart of E, F, G, & H color families,	37
3-3	Tonal ensembles yellow family,	38
3-4	Tonal ensembles orange family,	39
3-5	Tonal ensembles gray family,	40
3-6	Equal intensity collaboration/family crossing,	41
3-7	Equal intensity collaboration/family crossing,	42
3-8	Equal intensity collaboration/family crossing,	43
3-9	Multi intensity collaboration/family crossing,	45
3-10	Multi intensity collaboration/family crossing,	46
3-11	Multi intensity collaboration/family crossing,	47
4-1	Minimal and Maximal Focus techniques using scarves,	55
4-2	Minimal and Maximal Focus techniques using garments,	56
4-3	Tonal dressing variations,	59
4-4	Contrast dressing variations,	62
4-5	Print collaboration through Positive/Negative combinations,	64

4-6	Print collaboration variations,	66
4-7	Print collaboration variations,	68
4-8	Print collaboration variations,	71
4-9	Print mixing variations,	75
6-1	Singular coloration follow through/skirts,	89
6-2	Singular coloration follow through/pants,	91
6-3	Singular coloration follow through/prints,	93
6-4	Multiple coloration through repetition,	94
6-5	Multiple coloration through prints,	95
6-6	Color blocking,	96
6-7	Stylized color blocking,	97
6-8	Illusion formation through color blocking,	99
6-9	Stylized color blocking - bustline focus,	100
6-10	Stylized color blocking - hipline focus,	101
6-11	Illusion formation through fabric blocking,	103
6-12	Contoured belt usage,	105
6-13	Drop belts,	106
6-14	Sculptured belts,	107
6-15	Yoke/midriff treatment,	108
6-16	Buckle belts - definite "no"s,	110
6-17	Shoulder pads,	111
6-18	Silhouette blending,	113
6-19	Skirt lengths in relation to height,	114
6-20	Pant lengths in relation to height,	116
6-21	Princess lines,	117
6-22	Lines of asymmetry vertical,	118
6-23	Lines of asymmetry horizontal,	119
7-1	Thin neck illusion formation,	122
7-2	Long neck illusion formation,	123
7-3	Short neck illusion formation,	123

ILLUSTRATION INDEX

7-4   Sloping/narrow shoulders illusion formation, 124
7-5   Broad shoulders illusion formation, 125
7-6   Slim arms illusion formation, 126
7-7   Heavy arms illusion formation, 126
7-8   Long arms illusion formation, 127
7-9   Short arms illusion formation, 128
7-10 Top heavy illusion formation, 128
7-11 Flat chested illusion formation, 129
7-12 Short-waisted illusion formation, 130
7-13 Long-waisted illusion formation, 130
7-14 Thick waist illusion formation, 131
7-15 "Tummy ache" illusion formation, 132
7-16 Large hips illusion formation, 132
9-1   Suit cost analysis, 142

EUROFASHION: Unleashing The Designer In You

INDEX

A

A Passage to India, 26
"Absolutely Gorgeous" Concept, 78, 109
Accessories, 12, 28-30, 49, 80, 103-107, 109-112, 127-128
"Adoption-Related Confidence" principle, 22
Africa, 30, 122-123
Apparel, 135-146
    care, 144-146
    construction, 142-144
    layout, 141-143
    quality, 139-146
    sizing, 135-138
Architecture, 10-14
Arms, 80, 125-128
    heavy, 126
    long, 80, 127
    short, 127-128
    slim, 125-126
Asymmetric lines, 117-119
Attitude, 79-80

B

Belts, 103-109, 129
    buckle, 109
    contour, 104-105, 106-108, 129
    drop, 106
    sculptured, 107

BBW, *Big Beautiful Woman*, 150
Body Line, 87-107, 112-119, 122-133
    belts, 94, 103-107, 129
    color, 87-102
    fabric, 102-104
    forced direction, 94-100, 102-111
    style lines, 97, 112-119, 122-133
"Business" of Fashion, 14
Bustline, 98-102, 128-129
    flat, 129
    heavy, 128

C

Campbell, Naomi, 48
Cocktail Sportswear, 51
Color, 19, 24, 30-31, 34-52, 54-76, 87-128
    blocking, 88-102, 127-128
    combos, 36-48, 54-76
    cycle, 24-26, 30-31
    families, 34-52
    inspiration, 19
    personalities, 24, 34
    primary, 35
    secondary, 35
"Complement of Color", 72-76
Contour Belts, 104-108, 129
    drop, 106
    sculptured, 106
    yoke, 106, 108

INDEX

Contrast, 41-43, 44-47, 57-58, 60-63, 69, 110
Copycat Prints, 20-21
"Correlation of Print Size", 72-76
"Cosmetics", 48
Couture, 31

D
Daisy, 28
David, 88
"Degree of Contrast", 72-76
"Degree of Follow Through", 72-76
Demi Moore, 22
Donna Karan, 30, 88

E
Egypt, 12, 26
Emanuel Ungaro, 88
Environmental Influence, 27, 34
Ethnic Influence, 26
Evangelista, Linda, 22
Eveningwear, 14, 18

F
Fabric, 14-15, 20, 49-51, 102-104, 136, 142-144
    blocking, 102-104
    "hard", 51
    mixing, 49-51

    puffing, 15
    "soft", 51
    treatments, 50
Fashion
    "business", 14
    forecasters, 26
    "scale of importance", 24
Forced Direction, 94-100, 102

G
Geometric Influence, 12, 96
Glasses, 80
Gourmet Meal Influence, 14-22
Gulf Crisis, 31

H
Hair, 48-49
    pieces, 48-49
    wigs, 48-49
Hemlines, 31-32, 114-116
Hips, 80, 97, 99-102
    large, 80, 132-133
Hosiery, 109-110

I
Illusion Formation, 87-120, 122-133

INDEX

Influences, 10-21
    architecture, 10-14
    environmental, 10, 27, 34
    ethnic, 26
    gourmet, 14-21
    lingerie, 31
    social conscious awareness, 10, 28-29
    war, 31

J
Jewelry, 12, 29-30, 49
Jodphurs, 15, 30

K
Karan, Donna, 30, 88
Kimono Influences, 26
"Knee" point, 88-93, 114-116

L
Large Sizes, 78-80, 150
Layering, 112-114
Leonardo da Vinci, 88
Linda Evangelista, 22
Line, 88
    asymmetric, 117-119
    color, 87-102
    fabric, 102-104

focus, 88-120
style, 97, 112-119, 122-133
Lingerie, 31
"Love It Or Leave It" Test, 81-85

M
Madonna, 22, 31
influence, 31
Madras, 26
Manhattan Skyline Influence, 10-11
Maximal Focus Technique, 54-56
Michelangelo, 88
Minimal Focus Technique, 54-56
Moore, Demi, 22
Multiple Coloration, 88, 92-95

N
Naomi Campbell, 48
Neck
long, 122-123
short, 123
thin, 122

O
Out of Africa, 30

P

Paco Rabanne, 88
Pant, 31, 115
    palazzo, 115-116
    tapered, 116
Petites, 113-116
Point of Focus, 105-109
Positive/Negative, 63-65
Primary Colors, 35-44
Princess Line, 107, 117-119
Print(s), 20, 26, 57-58, 63-72, 72-76, 110
    collaboration, 57-58, 63-72, 110
    mixing, 57-58, 72-76, 110
    specialists, 26
Purchasing, 81-86

Q

Quality, 139-146

R

Rabanne, Paco, 88

S

Scarves, 54-57, 64-70, 104, 128
Scuba suit, 30
Sculptured, 42, 107
    belts, 107

    clothing, 42
    wigs, 48-49
Secondary Colors, 35-44
Sense of Independence, 79, 86, 150, 151
Shoulder(s), 97, 111-112, 124-125, 129
    broad, 125
    pads, 111-112, 124, 129
    sloping, 124
Silhouette, 10, 30, 122-133
Singular Coloration, 88-92
Sixties, 28, 31
Sizes, 78-80, 135-138
Skirts, 31, 112-115
    hobble, 31
    long, 31, 112-115
    short, 31, 112-115
Smart Shopper, 79-86
Social Consciousness, 28-29
Spanish Influence, 13
Sportswear, 14-15, 31, 51
Stomach, 104-110, 131-132
    bulge, 131-132
Style Lines, 97, 112-119, 122-123
Swatch, 20-21

T

Tailoring, 14-17
Taj Mahal, 10

INDEX

Textile, 14-15, 20, 24-32
    designer, 20
    forecaster, 24-32
    influences, 14-15, 20
    trends, 20
The Last Emperor, 26
The Last Supper, 88
Tonal, 38-40, 57-60, 110
Tower of Pisa, 10
Trapeze, 12
Trapunto, 15
Trends, 14-21, 24-26, 30, 48-49, 96
    clothing, 14-21, 30, 96, 137
    color, 19-21, 24-26, 30, 96
    cosmetic, 48
    hair, 48-49
    lingerie, 31
    scuba, 30
Twiggy (esque), 137

U
Ungaro, Emanuel, 88

V
Vietnam, 31

W

WWD, *Women's Wear Daily*, 150
Waist, 97-98, 103-107
    long, 130
    short, 129-130
    thick, 131
War, 31
    WWI, 31
    WWII, 31
    Gulf Crisis, 31
    Vietnam, 31
Wigs, 48-49

Photo by Sally G. Penny

Simran Preet Randhawa is an apparel design graduate of the Fashion Institute of Technology in New York. She has had the opportunity to work with many prestigious firms on a variety of levels in the fashion industry. Through extensive career travel, Simran has been involved in the design, construction, production, and marketing of quality garments for a variety of apparel firms in the United States and abroad. This, in turn, has led to awards in various design competitions.

Simran has also had the opportunity to make numerous television appearances. These appearances have led to regular spots as fashion commentator/consultant on several news and information programs.

Simran is currently head designer for Rajee', a better sportswear firm devoted to women size 12 to 26.

Having grown up in retail, Simran stays in touch on the retail level through a family owned specialty shop and shoe salon. Her knowledge and experience have established her as an authority in the areas of fashion and wardrobing.

Did you borrow this copy?

(Kindly photocopy this page.)

Order your own copy of *EUROFASHION...*
Unleashing The Designer In You.

Please send_____copies of *EUROFASHION...Unleashing The Designer In You* for $24.95 per copy, plus shipping/handling. (Shipping/handling: $3.00 for the first book; $1.00 each additional book)
(South Carolina residents add 6% sales tax.)
(Outside the United States, prices slightly higher)

***For shipment of additional books to different addresses, kindly provide full information (name, address, phone, and gift card).

PAYMENT:
_____ Check or Money Order
_____ Credit Card (Circle One)
       Visa, MasterCard, AMEX, Discover

Credit Card Information:
Card number:_____
Name on card:_____Exp. date:_____
Signature:_____
Shipping Address:_____

Please allow two to three weeks for orders to reach you.

Orders should be directed to:

Immis Publishing
102 Sharon Street
Suite 310-A
Bamberg, S.C. 29003
(803) 245-0146

Announcement of future publications . . .

ACCESSORI ARTISTRI --- An illustrative guide to the world of accessories. Discover new uses for all types of accessories. Learn new techniques of creating accessories through the use of ordinary household items. **Explore the next level of Eurofashion.**

ACCESSORI ARTISTRI...Scarves And The Like --- Are you one of those people that loves scarves but has no idea what to do with them? Discover hundreds of new ways of tying and using scarves and the like. Through clear, in-depth illustrations, become an expert and "wow" your friends and family.

If you wish to be kept informed of our future publications, send us your name, address, and phone number for our mailing lists.

Send information to:

Immis Publishing
102 Sharon Street
Suite 310-A
Bamberg, S.C. 29003